I0006792

Pass Your IT Certification Exam the First Time : Tips and Tricks for Success

By William A. Cellich

CISSP, CEH, AIIM ECM Master, Microsoft MCTS

and many, many more

Copyright 2012-2015 © CCS Productions and William A.

Cellich.

All Rights Reserved.

TABLE OF CONTENTS

NOTICE: All product and company names referenced or listed herein are trademarks™ or registered® trademarks of their respective holders. Use of them does not imply any affiliation with or endorsement by them.

Preface

So, just who is this guy, and why should I listen to him about taking certification exams? Fair enough...

It all started a long time ago, in a galaxy far, far....ummmm.
No.
Scratch that.

Once upon a time, there was this man who decided to embark upon a Quest for Enlightenment...
Nope.

There was this one time, in band camp....ummm.
Never mind.

Knock, knock.
Who's there?
Opportunity.

Okay. Enough with the warm-up jokes. This is serious business, right?

I know what you might be thinking:

" I just dropped some hard –earned coin to find out how you can nuke this certification thing, and this guy thinks he is Jerry Seinfeld or Louis C.K.? What gives?"

During your career as an Information Technology Professional, you will face many challenges. Getting out of your chosen major in college with a decent GPA is one of these things. Finding a first job is another challenge, especially today. Career moves, both planned and unplanned, can throw your best laid plans right into the circular file.

Throughout all these trial and tribulations, it helps to develop some perspective, and the first thing to assist you with developing that is a sense of humor.

So, lighten up for a minute. We will cover the serious stuff soon enough.

I started out my work life as a dishwasher. I quickly progressed from being a boy able to slide greasy junk from a plate into a garbage disposal into a man who knew what to do with a mop and broom. I could break down a box with the best of them, and woes betide anyone who thought they could rinse down the pots and pans better or faster than me. I soon exhausted the challenge of deciphering the contents of the just-ingested meals that people had consumed, based solely on the mangled remnants of dessert, the coffee cups filled with lipstick stained cigarette butts, and the barely touched escargot remains.[1]

---

[1] I had been informed by one of the other dishwashers that these were considered delicacies. Steve Martin and I tended to agree that they were merely a plateful of snails. My co-worker, however, never missed the opportunity to snack on these leftovers before he slipped the cleared plate into the washing machine rack to be power cleansed.

My next job was working in a bookstore in a shopping mall that has since been demolished. I really enjoyed that job, as I was able to get a LOT of reading done. And, it also was close to the college, where I was beginning my educational journey to become a chemist.

The bookstore job is one I fondly remember. I also fondly remember telling my supervisor I was leaving, because the hours and wages barely covered my expenses.

She told me "Don't let the door hit you in the ..."
Actually, she wished me luck. I think.

I did a brief holiday stint at UPS. The first day on the job I dropped an 80 pound box of iron I-beam onto my big toe, and sheared off the toenail. I learned the valuable lesson of wearing steel-toed boots.

When the season ended, I was unemployed. But at least my toenail had grown back.

I then moved on to my next career move – assistant plumber.

I learned all about how toilets and bidets work, how to install a dishwasher, garbage disposal, water heater, etc.

I also learned how to use an acetylene torch to solder copper pipe without setting fire to a wooden cabinet, (and how to put out the inevitable fires that naturally happened from burning wooden cabinets with an acetylene torch, when all you had was a can of Pepsi).

I dug ditches in the rain, (uphill - both ways), and then dropped in the PVC pipe for sprinklers and drains, getting pretty looped from the cement fumes and other wonderful chemical smells associated with plumbing.

But, there was something lacking in that job, to my young and eager mind.

Somehow, assuring you and your loved ones could poop in relative comfort, and take a nice bath or shower without worrying about the water backing up, really didn't balance out the fact that this was another low-paying position.[2]

My next attempt at trying to figure out what to do when I grew up was to become a Postal Letter Carrier. That lasted about a year. My, the stories I could tell... but I digress.

At this point, I was offered a position as chief cook and bottle washer for a defense contractor.

I ended up spending almost twenty years there.

---

[2] I learned some VERY useful things during that one year or so of plumbing. It has served me well over the years. I almost NEVER call a plumber, choosing to wait until things are REALLY out of control until I do.

During that time, I was able to score two Bachelor's degrees, some Master's level college courses in Computer Information Systems, and a few patents for jet engines.

I worked on the Space Shuttle LOX Turbopump and other advanced rocket engines, such as the RL-10 and did things I am still not allowed to talk about. In 1995, I created one of the first Record Management Systems for storage and retrieval of Non-Conformance Reports for rocket engines, worked with lasers, Scanning Electron Microscopes, FTIR and other chemical analytic equipment, and other cool-sounding devices.

In 1996, I founded a user group for the then-new Microsoft Access 2.0 database program, and facilitated one of the first LANs that allowed Solaris and Windows NT 3.51 to transfer Unigraphics II CAD files and data.[3]

---

[3] I ended up giving a presentation to an group of engineers at the Space Camp, in Huntsville, Alabama. My clearest recollection of that time is of me, wearing a business suit, riding the "Ejection Seat" ride, and shooting several hundred feet into the air, strapped into a little bench with this flimsy seat belt.

I ended up as some kind of expert in Classified Computer Systems, which falls into that category of not being able to talk about it too much.

That job led to my going to work as an expert in Document Imaging System administration. After four years of THAT, I moved into consulting.

During this long period of time I also amassed so many certifications that it boggles my mind to even think about how much time I devoted to getting them.
We are talking, SUN Solaris, MS ACCESS, vendor certifications, specific certs needed to perform Department of Defense work, certifications that no longer exist, certifications that proved of limited career value, and certifications such as the CISSP.

The thing that interests me now is looking back and trying to understand my motivations – what exactly was it that sent me on that particular path? I mean, pretty women, money, fame and power, sure...but what else?

For me, I suppose it is the love of learning new things, but it is also the validation that I KNOW these new things well enough to pass a pretty thorough examination of my skills.

Now, things were not always rosy regarding passing courses, or exams. I started out with NO system of how to study, and I paid some heavy prices, such as retesting, and missing out on cool beta programs from Microsoft and other vendors. It never really seemed to be that big a deal, because I was still doing other cool things.

But, one day, I added up the cost in time and money, and resolved that I would become *SERIOUS* about getting these done.[4]

So, I applied some of my experience into a system of study that proved very successful in allowing me to pass certification exams the FIRST time.

---

[4] I told you we would get to the serious stuff soon enough, right?

Exams for certifications that are fairly well-respected in the Information Technology world. Certifications that almost everyone would love to have on their resume:

CISSP

CEH

AIIM **Enterprise** **Content** **Management** (Practitioner, Specialist and Master)

ASP.NET MCTS

... and many more. [5]

What you now hold in your hands is the distillation of the amassed knowledge of someone who has walked the walk, trod the certification path down many avenues, and then put into practice those arcane bits and pieces of what seems trivial nonsense in his everyday work.

I **had** to get some of these, and I decided I wanted to get others.

---

[5] About forty at last count...

I paid for many out-of-pocket, and managed to finagle a few from my various employers. (I feel they all got their money's worth, incidentally.)

It is my hope that the information here will do three things:

1. Help you to choose certifications that are valuable to YOU.
2. Provide some perspective regarding the value of IT certifications in general.
3. Show you a better way to prepare and then pass the exams.

Let's get started –

<*>

Introduction

The employment market is very challenging today.

If you have a good job, currently, you should consider yourself fortunate. There are many people who were employed recently and then suddenly found themselves out of work after fairly considerable and notable careers. People lose their jobs due to no fault of their own, are laid off, or through illness or other circumstances.

The traditional work paradigms are gone. Loyalty seems to be a rare commodity on both sides of the employer /employee equation.

If you have just graduated high school, or even college, the opportunities available may be few. No longer can one count on a lifetime career, or continued employment with just one employer.

The existence of right-to-work legislation, outsourcing, and the need for ever more efficiency in business has led to the most competitive work environment in almost forty years. The extensive use of information technologies such as the Internet and other business software, coupled with a need to reduce costs has led to fewer jobs being available.

It is very important to maintain a positive outlook and continue to try to meet the requirements of the employers that are hiring.

As you already know, Human Resource departments are becoming more Darwinian in determining who even gets an interview. Job seekers are forced to go through a gauntlet of seemingly impossible criteria as HR goes through tens or even hundreds of resumes trying to find the best candidates and fit for each job.

The rise of automated systems that parse your resume make it critical that the information and skills you are selling are relevant, current, and applicable to that particular set of business problems.

Therefore, it is more important than ever that you stand out.

Whether you are an experienced professional currently employed, a newbie, have found yourself suddenly unemployed, or are in school and planning on a career in Information Technology, you must begin NOW to assure a better and more positive future for yourself.

For many, this means getting certified in a particular area.

‹ ❄ ›

The Audience for This Information

The techniques discussed here are applicable to many learning experiences.

If you are seeking a certification in a field other than Information Technology, there is generic information that will aid you in understanding the strategy of testing, and also help you determine your personal learning style.

However, the primary focus will be on popular and recognized Information Technology certifications.

While we will not delve too deeply into the particulars of a given certification path, there are some similarities that we will examine.

The information in this book will help you regardless of where in your career path you are situated.

Career Path Milestones –

You have several milestones as you progress in a career, and the information that follows is geared to helping you, regardless of where in your career path you find yourself at any given moment:

- Newbies
- First Job Holders
- If Certification Is Necessary to Keep Your Current Position
- Middle Managers
- Directors
- Consultants

Newbies –

If this is your first certification experience, you will be able to take the methods and techniques found in this book and apply them to your other coursework.

The process of learning does not have to be a grind.

You can use this new knowledge to build a system of learning that will provide a strong foundation that will serve you well as you continue your career path or paths.

At this point, practical experience is usually the area in which you are weak.

Even if you have been building PCs or hacking since your teen years, being able to successfully integrate your '1337 h@x0r skilz' into a work environment can be challenging.

The pursuit of certification performs two important duties that allow you stand out from your peers:

- It shows you can follow direction[6]
- It shows you respect the organizational culture

To get in the door, you must follow certain rules. You need to be able to take direction, and also, unfortunately, to conform to cultural standards.

Sure, you can join a start-up where they shoot each other with foam missiles, have coding marathons full of caffeine and fun, and generally goof around while you produce the next 'killer app'.

_____

[6] Notice that I did not say 'directions'. Anyone can be a cook, but becoming a master chef requires a completely different set of skills, and you can develop those only in an environment in which you have established mutual respect.

But, those situations are few and far between, and you need to have proven your chops to even be approached for membership.

The vast majority of jobs require a mind-numbing array of paperwork, orientation, and the ability to fit in with the culture.

Certifications may provide the necessary credentials to a prospective employer that you know how to 'play the game'. And, they will at least get you in front of HR.

First Job –

Once you have obtained employment, the value of continuing to add to your skill set is obvious. People succeed in organizations by providing value to the employer, and one way to highlight that value is to obtain relevant certifications. For example, if you are an Information Security Professional, you may notice many job opportunities will stipulate that you "need to be certified pursuant to DoD 8570".

This means you need to have one or more of the certifications as listed in the directive.

If you perform a cursory review of the DoD Directive, you will encounter this chart (Defense, Department of, 2012) (Defense, Department of, 2012):

Table AP3.T2. DoD Approved Baseline Certifications

IAT Level I	IAT Level II	IAT Level III
A+-CE Network+CE SSCP	GSEC Security+CE SSCP	CISA GCIH GSE CISSP (or Associate)

IAM Level I	IAM Level II	IAM Level III
CAP GISF GSLC Security+CE	CAP GSLC CISM CISSP (or Associate)	GSLC CISM CISSP (or Associate)

IASAE I	IASAE II	IASAE III
CISSP (or Associate)	CISSP (or Associate)	CISSP - ISSEP CISSP - ISSAP

CNDSP Analyst	CNDSP Infrastructure Support	CNDSP Incident Responder	CNDSP Auditor	CNDSP Manager
GCIA CEH GCIH	SSCP CEH	GCIH CSIH CEH	CISA GSNA CEH	CISSP-ISSMP CISM

This is a listing of the applicable certifications required for these positions, as Information Assurance professionals working on Department of Defense contracts.[7]

This list includes the CompTIA Plus series, the CEH, CISSP, and SANS / GSEC and other SANS certifications of various flavors.

Many job descriptions may indicate that you either already possess these, or you must be willing to obtain certification within six months.[8]

---

[7]Refer to:
http://iase.disa.mil/eta/iawip/content_pages/iabaseline.html for the full Directive.

[8] An assumption that must be made with regard to this is that you now have some experience to back up the pursuit of these certifications. Especially pertaining to the CISSP, you cannot even sit for some of these exams unless you can provide documented evidence and be able to supply references to vouch for that experience. Therefore, the CISSP more accurately is placed in the Middle Manager Audience, but there may be individuals for whom these circumstances may apply at this juncture.

With the information you will learn shortly, that should be a realistic goal.

If Certification Is Required to Maintain Your Position –

This is indeed a rather anxiety ridden situation in which to find oneself. Your company may have been folded into another, or there is a restructuring occurring, or you may have been given a directive by your supervisor or manager that you absolutely MUST get certified.

It won't matter that you have ten or more years of experience at this point, or that you are the only person who can still perform the arcane functions needed to program the AS400 to spit out TPS reports. When the edict comes down from on-high, your choice is clear – get certified, or polish up that resume.

Your goal here is to negotiate a reasonable amount of time for preparation, and hopefully get the employer to foot the bill for a boot camp or at least the exam fee.[9]

I am not going to mince words here – if I was in this situation, (and I have been), boot camps by far are the most expedient route.

I will address the advantages and disadvantages of each approach in more detail in an upcoming chapter.

There is a definite approach to use, even regarding boot camps.

By using the techniques you will learn shortly, you will improve your odds for success, even under these difficult circumstances.

―――――――――――――――――――――

[9] Getting them to buy this e-book for you was a very smart decision on your part! If you bought it yourself, ask your accountant if it is TAX DEDUCTIBLE!

Middle Manager –

In this situation, you are likely having to obtain certification because of regulatory or compliance issues, or because you are simply interested in getting certified. Your options are more than likely being offered in a more relaxed atmosphere (although not necessarily) and you can take time to self-pace or distance learn, perhaps even participating during office hours.

You already know the value of certification, either from your experiences in hiring personnel, or by leveraging your existing certifications to gain your position.

You may even feel passionately that certifications are even worthless, or do not accurately map to real world work skills, but are being pressured to only hire certified people. Because of this, it may have been made clear to you that actually HAVING those certifications yourself would give some weight to understanding their value to the organization. (So you may actually be in the situation described previously as needing these certifications to keep YOUR job!)

Regardless of the underlying motivations, you can rest assured that by using the strategies you will soon learn that you will be able to perform well in obtaining these certifications.

Director –

Being a Director or Chief of an organization has its own set of problems that will not be thoroughly addressed during our discussion. This is outside our scope of certifications tips and tricks.

One thing to remember, however, is that you may be tasked with managing personnel who are attempting to succeed in your organization, and their ability to successfully obtain required certifications is due in large part to how you provide support. Employees who are required to get certified may find themselves in a confused and frightened state, or anxious about their future.

Change management is a very important component and a constant stressor in most businesses today.

Therefore, being able to alleviate their concerns about how well an employee feels they are able to perform by providing a strong message of assisting their efforts is tantamount to achieving organizational cohesion. [10]

―――――――――――――――――――

[10] I have been in various places during my career where I had very strong support for my endeavors, and the supervisor or manager would bend over backwards to accommodate unusual or flexible work schedules. As long as I did my part, and managed to finish my work in a timely and satisfactory manner, they would allow me to pursue my education, and certification efforts.

On the other hand, I have been in organizations where, even though I was brought in as an expert and we decided as a group that certain additional training was necessary, the fact of my being a consultant limited my ability to join in on that training.

As a result, I now include in my contracts a clause that I will be allowed to attend one boot camp per contracted session, at the expense of the Client, as part of my compensation package. This is a win / win, in that I am able to continue to remain certified with relevant training, and the Client may realize certain tax or other financial advantages that affect their budget.

Consultant –

As a consultant, you are probably very familiar with the marketing advantages of having a widely recognized certification backing your experience. Particularly with networking certifications such as the Cisco certs, there are very real advantages.

Many Fortune 500 companies will not hire non-certified consultants because of the risk of errors causing substantial financial loss.

However, as a consultant, the necessity of obtaining certifications that are both current and relevant can be an expensive venture. [11] I have found it advantageous to either partner with referral companies that can negotiate a training budget into your proposal, or to arrange to attend corporate training that is being offered during upgrades, migrations, or re-engineering of a company.

_____

[11] I know of one consultant to IBM who spent over $150,000 in one year in getting relevant certifications and partnership agreements.

You may not always be able to get this training, but most companies are more than happy to give you a benefit in lieu of a paycheck. It comes from a different category of expenses and budget money, so there are definite advantages for them to do so. Usually you will have to ask for it, as it is not a default 'go-to' option for compensation.

Many companies will outright tell you that you will not qualify for training because you are NOT an employee. This can work to your advantage, in that you can then honestly adjust your rates upward to accommodate the certification. If you do this in a competitive manner, you can still achieve your goal of certification. [12]

One thing to remember for all of these career points is that you will be required to maintain your certifications.

---

[12] That is to say, don't gouge the Client with your training costs. You can incorporate the cost into your other expenses, and adjust in other areas such as lodging or meals. Of course, if you find yourself in a special situation where the demand is very high for your particular skill set, then you can shoot for the moon. The Client can only say "No", after all.

You may have to study articles on the subject matter and take quizzes, or attend seminars to stay relevant on the latest trends in your field.

Continuing education is a necessity to assure your skills are relevant, and also indicative that you are serious and motivated to show that you are improving your understanding of information technology.

As you are soon going to realize, certification is not an end, it is just the beginning.

What This Book Can Do For You

This information is a distillation of techniques and advice I gained through many long years of schooling, decades of work experience, consulting, and sitting exams.

It is AN approach that worked for me.

Since I have quite a collection of certifications, and have had some success in my career, it occurred to me to share my experiences with others to assist them in obtaining their certifications.

By using the methods I have used, there is probably a better than average chance of passing a given certification exam.

This book is NOT information about specific questions regarding any particular certification.

There are plenty of resources out there for the motivated individual to peruse at their leisure.

Additionally, I am bound by the terms and conditions of most if not all of the Certification Bodies that have granted me the certifications to NOT disclose specific questions regarding those particular exams.

However, you will find a lot of good resources, techniques, tricks and tips that will allow you to perform much better in a given situation when sitting an exam.

What This Book Can't Do For You

It can't **make** you study. It won't write the correct answers to any of the certification exams down for you. It won't do the heavy lifting of having to do the exercises in your study material.

REMEMBER – IT IS UP TO YOU.

I am **not** giving you a way to cheat the exam. I am teaching you a way to study material so that you will be confident when you approach ANY exam, or test, and be able to account for yourself accordingly.

If you use the techniques I will show you, you may be able to undo some bad habits you have picked up during your 'education'.

A Short Digression

I cannot nor would I guarantee you will pass EVERY certification exam for which you sit. That is not possible, as I do not know how much effort any one individual will put into obtaining their certification.

But I would like to present you with a story that may give you some of that valuable perspective that I have mentioned, and why you may find it worth your time to read and absorb this material.

This small tale has to do with my tutoring experiences. I have had very good, even exceptional results, from my students whom I have tutored. I have been teaching technical information since early 2000, and that includes several years of training adults as well as teenagers.

My usual students were interested in mathematics, or chemistry, or physics, or computer applications.

In every case where my students have achieved success it was because THEY applied themselves.

Each one learned the basics of the techniques I am laying out here. Each performed to their best ability.
Of course, I can point to a few failures, but in each case I feel they did not succeed because they did not apply themselves.[13]

The point I am making is that, even if you are given a method for success, and even the exact answers for a particular exam, for that matter, if you do not make an effort to learn the material, you will most assuredly NOT pass your tests.

This fact may seem obvious on face value, but life has a way of providing many distractions, and a lot of the time you may feel justified in procrastinating.

---

[13]I am not blaming them. There were extenuating circumstances in many cases. They simply would not or could
not study. It was not a matter of intelligence; it was one of not doing the work.

But, I would like to present to you one very instructive example of just what can be achieved if one is ready to learn, and motivated enough to succeed.

Against all odds...

Some time ago, I was tutoring a female student who was studying to complete her GED.[14]

She had left school, a few years earlier, and wanted to obtain the GED to get gainful employment.

We had a very large amount of information to cover, and only a few weeks to do so.

I would go to her house to help her prepare for the exam.

She was scheduled to sit the exam in late summer, and it was already July.

---

[14] Scoff if you like about the GED. I feel very strongly about its value to certain members of our society, and would go toe to toe with anyone who feels it is inferior to a 'real' High School diploma.

Using the methods I am going to describe here, she studied and did homework.

I corrected it, assigned more problems, and worked with her closely to get her ready.

She sat the exam, and we found out in late September that she had passed.

I was elated.

BECAUSE –

- She was living with her parents, who were divorcing
- She had a three month old baby that required her attention
- She was a single mother
- Her brother used to do drugs and jump from the second story of the house into the backyard pool while we were studying, among other outlandish behaviors
- Her friends were constantly trying to get her to come out and 'play'
- She was nineteen years old and in charge of her own life
- ***BUT SHE DID NOT MAKE EXCUSES***

When we were doing the multiplication tables, I noticed that every time she was doing 3 times 9, she would say "28", and not the correct answer of "27".

The first time this occurred, I gently corrected her, and we moved onto the next problem.

The fourth or fifth time it had happened, I knew that someone had TOLD her that 3*9 = 28.

They had cemented that into her memory.

And, all this time she had **believed** this was the correct answer.

So, I did the following for her:

For homework, I asked her to write out the times tables from 1x1=1 to 12x12=144.

By hand.

Before our next session (about two days).

Then, the next time I was there, while she would work on problems, I corrected any errors on the times tables she had made. (Yep, 3*9 = 28 was there. Among others.)

At the end of the day, I handed her the times tables back, with my corrections.

For homework, I again asked her to **copy** the corrected times tables, from 1x1=1 to 12x12=144.

Ten times.

By hand.

Before our next session (about two days).

When I returned to our next session, I examined all of the work she had done. It was accurate. There was no 3*9=28 this time.

Nor were there any other errors.

I verbally quizzed her and she responded correctly 3*9=27 without any hesitation.

(She aced the GED math quiz, incidentally. 98% if I recall.)

Why am I sharing this story with you?

YOU HAVE NO EXCUSES.

If this young woman could pass an important exam under some of the worst learning conditions I have ever seen, then **you** should be able to use these techniques and succeed as well.

I don't assume that you may have your own set of problems to which you need to attend. We all do.

I am going to challenge you to overcome all of the obstacles in your thinking about why you CAN'T do it just this second:

- Your baby is crying
- Your spouse / significant other / squeeze needs you for <fill in the blank>[15]
- You are too tired
- The <house – car – kids – dog – cat – horse> is dirty and needs cleaned
- You already worked all day
- You deserve a rest
- Your other children have homework to do
- The bills need paid
- This is too hard
- I am not smart enough to do this
- It's not really that big a deal if I do this in the morning
- <CREATE YOUR OWN WHINY BABY EXCUSE HERE – I WILL WAIT—I HAVE GOT ALL THE TIME IN THE WORLD!>

---

[15] This blank is most probably sex, incidentally.

Remember the **most** important lesson in life:

TANSTAAFL   ---

Otherwise known as:

THERE AIN'T NO SUCH THING AS A FREE LUNCH![16]

Learn to prioritize.[17]

---

[16] Thanks go to Mr. Robert A. Heinlein, the Dean of Science Fiction, for first concretely putting this concept into writing in "The Moon Is A Harsh Mistress". You must put in effort in order to derive satisfactory results.

[17] Say, do you need to get a GED? I know a nice young lady that can probably make some time to tutor you.

Why Get Certified?

There are several obvious reasons to get an IT certification. [18]

- Validation of skills

- Recognition of expertise in a specific IT specialty

- Regulatory requirements

- To keep one's current job

- Staying current with new technology

- Personal sense of accomplishment

While this list is not complete, it gives the main reasons most people would pursue certification.

---

[18] For purpose of our discussion, the focus will be on currently recognized Information Technology certifications. The methods that are illustrated will also work for many other areas of study.

Obstacles to Getting Certified

Some of the obstacles to attaining certification include:

- Lack of knowledge of the particular skills required to pass
- Too much time has elapsed since the skills were last used
- Procrastination
- Self-confidence is low
- Time management skills are poor
- Unfocused approach to learning
- Everyday distractions in your life

Which certifications are best?

This is the $164,000 question.

The best certification for YOU to have is not necessarily the one you MUST have. Carefully examine your need and motivations for getting certified, reflecting on the information already presented.

Certification can be an expensive undertaking, in both time and money, and may put a strain on personal relationships while you are preparing. If your job depends on a specific IT Certification, (such as CISSP) then you may be faced with a difficult choice. [19]

---

[19] Some certifications have specific experience criteria, and may require someone who is already certified to vouch for you. This is the case for the CISSP. In some cases, experience criteria are very strictly checked, and you cannot even sit for the exam without evidence of this experience.

The requirements for these certifications vary.

Certifications can be divided into the following categories:

- Vendor Specific
- Vendor Neutral
- IT Professional Skills
- Compliance and Regulatory

Let us take a moment to examine each one of these more closely:

Vendor Specific –

The certifications here are usually for software programs, such as Microsoft or Linux operating systems, or in hardware products, such as particular Cisco routers, or Checkpoint firewalls. These can include certifications for programming languages as well, such as JAVA or .NET.

The Adobe software certifications and many of the companies that sell software for Enterprise Content Management (ECM), Enterprise Resource Planning (ERP), and Customer Relations Management Systems (CRM or CRMS) all have certification paths to address the specific level of expertise required.

Most start with a Foundational series, and gradually increase difficulty from System Administration, to Developer, and Expert. Examples of these are the Microsoft SharePoint certifications, SAP and Kofax certifications, and EMC Captiva / Input Accel certifications. [20]

ORACLE database certifications are an example of a specific product that has a defined certification path.

---

[20] An excellent resource that I have used was Anne Martinez "Getting Certified to Get Ahead". This book gives a comprehensive review of almost every major IT certification out there. However, the last reliable date I can find for publishing is 2000. It is still available, though dated.

There are also in-house certs available from many companies - Apple, Dell, EMC, HP, IBM and pretty much any Line of Business application made. [21]

Many of these certs are to assist service providers or partners with market differentiation and advertising credentials, and are requirements to be able to participate in their various tiers of benefits.[22]

Vendor Neutral –

These certifications are offered by organizations such as CompTIA, and include the "Plus" series (A+, Network +, Security +, etc.) or may be for specific areas or markets.

---

[21] Again, a complete list is not within the scope of this book. A quick Google search will usually provide a list of relevant certification topics.

[22] More details are available on the websites for a specific vendor. It is a simple matter of typing "training", "certifications" or "education" into their on-site search engine for more information.

Since many people outside of the United States of America[23] may be sitting for some of these exams, be sure to check your local regulations and requirements for your qualifications to sit for the test.

IT Professional Skills –

The certifications here are usually for software programs, such as Adobe Professional products, or vertically targeted software, such as is used for specialized purposes, such as image capture, Optical Character Recognition, or in specific hardware products, such as for networking.

Hacking skills are also in this group, such as SANS GIAC, OWASP, and CEH certifications.

---

[23] Did you not know that there is ANOTHER United States? Have you ever heard of the "Estados Unidos de Mexico"?

Compliance and Regulatory –

These certifications are used to establish a conformance to a regulatory contractual requirement. This would include CISA, ISO certifications, or even CISSP.

The important thing here is to find the certification path that suits your interests and career path the closest.

⊰ ❋ ⊱

Learning Styles[24]

People typically have a style of learning that suits them best. Recognized learning styles include:

- Visual
- Auditory
- Tactile or Kinesthetic

Let's take a look at each for a more detailed explanation of each style .

Visual –

People who learn using visual cues are referred to as 'visual' learners.

———————————————

[24] (Visual, Auditory, and Kinesthetic Learning Styles (VAK), 2011)

Visual learners can recall information better when it is presented using charts, graphs, or colorful pictures or examples.

They may draw memory maps, doodles, or other pictures to help them to organize and understand material. They may also learn simply by watching a video or even someone else perform tasks.

Auditory-

People who gain understanding of material from listening to the spoken word, or associating sounds with their learning are referred to as 'auditory' learners.

Auditory learners may recall information by listening to music while learning. They may learn through tapes, or audio books, or even by playing back recordings made during lectures.

Tactile-

People who touch or perform hands-on activities to learn are referred to as 'tactile' learners. This is also known as kinesthetic, or motion, learning.

The act of moving the body and hands produces a muscle memory that stimulates the memory to recall specific information or remember data.

Tactile learners prefer to 'do it themselves', often gaining a very thorough understanding of the material after only one session. They may build things to cement their understanding, or take them apart to more readily understand the functions of specific parts or processes.

Writing is also considered a tactile event, so they may make copious notes while observing learning activities.

Of course, most of us use various combinations of these styles during our lives.

But, *when you are studying to take an exam*, you must be aware of styles that impede your ability as well as those that accentuate your learning.

Your Personal Learning Style –

To get the best results regarding how you are going to perform on exams, you are going to have put some effort and take some time to actually record how you study, and the results of the ways that you study.

This is not to side-step the methods I am showing you; it is to understand which of these will be a better fit for your personality, demeanor and even the demands on your time.

Some of the methods we will use are simple tricks, like mnemonics, but others require more concentration to the task at hand.

A positive outcome for you, as a learner, is not only to remember the materials being studied long enough for passing the test, but also to carry it forward into long-term memory where you will be able to recall and apply it on the job.

For instance, listening to loud music might be fun, but unless you can demonstrate an increase in your test scores with a valid double blind test, it is probably doubtful that in your case it is doing anything other than providing a distraction to concentrating on your studies.

However, the same music at a lower volume may indeed produce an environment conducive to allowing you to retain critical information.[25]

_____

[25] This is one area in which you are going to have to experiment. If you do, you should note both the duration and volume of the music, the type of information you are studying, and other variables such as whether you have taken medication, are drinking anything (alcoholic or non-alcoholic), if you are ill, or how much sleep you have been getting. The day of the tests, you will need to reproduce the conditions as closely as possible, trying not to vary too many of the factors at once. There are lots of studies out there on the Interwebs to provide data about this, but the only thing that really matters is how YOU react to additional stimuli, while studying. If a quiet library is where you do your best studying, go there. If you like to pound Monster Energy drinks and listen to Metalocalypse at full volume, who am I to criticize that method if you consistently can perform in those conditions? (However, in most cases that would qualify as an outlier.)

This self-examination will not occur overnight. You are going to have to track the times when you feel you are studying well, and compare the actual test results against the criteria you are monitoring.

In this regard, the CBT software or online sites will provide a very easy method to at least gauge your progress, but they only are telling part of the story.

If you pass an A+ simulated exam with 85%, for instance, the software will indicate the areas in which you require more practice.

But, it does not measure how tired you were, or hungry, or worried, or distracted by family matters or other personal issues, if you were drunk or sober, or thirsty, or horny or anything else other than an objective metric of you answered these questions correctly, and you didn't answer those ones correctly.

This is not something to take lightly.

REPEATABLE QUALITY PERFORMANCE IN ANY ENDEAVOR REQUIRES STABILITY OF THE CONTROLLABLE VARIABLES.

What I am saying is that if you take the same test, under identical conditions, you SHOULD get almost identical results.

The difference in how you study is the most important factor, in my opinion, as to predictable success.

Examination Traps -

I have studied in a large variety of conditions. When I was much younger and in college, I devoted a large amount of study time to other endeavors, such as socializing.

This did not serve me well come time to take the exams.

I was used to a fairly easy studying routine, and I also was lucky enough to be able to pass exams with high marks with little actual hard work.

However, the socializing took its toll, and I ended up having to cover lost ground. Coupled with working a full-time job, this presented a daunting challenge to getting passing grades.

When I decided to finally buckle down and STUDY, I carved out time to manage my workload more effectively. [26]

I would set aside a specific amount of time, in a specific area of my room; with particular care as to lighting and made sure I did not have to move from that spot except to relieve myself.

The interesting thing was that this also translated into better habits at work. I became more organized, and was able to produce better outcomes in less time, because I developed work habits that built upon one another, rather than having to run around trying to find relevant information.

Now, many of you reading this are rolling your eyes, or saying to yourself "Big deal. So you developed a way to schedule your time. Whoopee."

---

[26] In fact one of the courses I took taught time-management techniques. Which I am now sharing with you!

In reality, **VERY FEW PEOPLE** learn these skills at any stage of their education.

Fewer still formally are taught that there is a specific order to gathering your information, classifying it logically, and then analyzing it for trends and then being able to use that to create logical inferences and deductions about complex problems.

In fact, I was almost thirty years old when I took advantage of that time management class, and it paid huge dividends going forward.

If you have taken scientific or mathematic courses in college, then you develop logical ways of thinking about those kinds of problems.

For certification exams, this is not necessarily considered a strength.

One of the interesting things about these tests is that they will phrase certain questions to create 'fuzzy' situations.

For instance you may get a problem such as this:

Which of the following applies to an operating system:

  a) They need security software to prevent viruses

  b) They need security software to prevent infection by malware

  c) A firewall is adequate protection for your operating system

  d) UNIX is somewhat secure against viruses

  e) All of the above

Without actually knowing the context of this question, and the exam on which it is usually found, we can take a few logical guesses.

First, what IS an operating system?

Windows, Linux, and the Mac OS are all operating systems, but there is also UNIX, (and all its wonderful flavors), mainframe and embedded operating systems, and even cell phones use them (Android).

There are a lot of conflicting possibilities in the question.

- Is a firewall REALLY adequate protection? What do we know about firewalls?
- How do viruses actually work?
- Is malware a kind of virus or something else entirely?
- Is it true that UNIX is somewhat secure against viruses?
- Is ALL of that true?

If you had to choose just ONE answer, which is the best one?[27]

The question might also be presented as follows:

Select ALL of the following that apply to an operating system:
    a) They need security software to prevent viruses
    b) They need security software to prevent infection by malware
    c) A firewall is adequate protection for your operating system
    d) UNIX is somewhat secure against viruses
    e) All of the above

---

[27] Welcome to the world of the CISSP exam.

The answer here may seem more apparent:

A, B, and maybe C

If you picked A and B, you KNOW those are true statements. C is maybe not so cut and dried, right?

The rub is that D is the only **correct** answer.

That is because the other answers depend on a broad assumption as to what an operating system is, and how viruses work.

C is a logical way of thinking, but many items that don't use firewalls work just fine without them (such as embedded software in vending machines or Point of Sale systems).

Many exams operate on nuances as to how the questions are phrased, and are designed to be confusing. The exam makers need to be sure that they are testing your knowledge of the subject and not your ability for rote memorization.

Herein lies the caution for most of you taking certification exams without the requisite experience:

You need to understand the QUESTION being asked, before you can provide the best ANSWER.

And, herein lies the caution for most of you taking certification exams with the requisite experience:

Do not OVER THINK the problem.

On some certification exams you are required to write your answers in essay form. You need to be able to succinctly identify the key ideas as stated in the problem, and respond with logically sound answers to each point.

When we know a lot about a subject, there is a tendency to gloss over or assume important information already has been stated or provided to us. Context is an important factor in being able to perform well on certification exams.

This applies whether the exam is a multiple choice, essay, or fill in the blank exam, but not so much to actual laboratory simulations.

In lab sims, there is a fairly defined way of getting to the end result, and you either get there correctly or you don't.

You may have to try several approaches, and if you end up running out of time, it did not mean you did not have AN answer, but probably more likely did not have the most EFFICIENT answer.

This is a pitfall of lab sims, and the best way to combat that is with practical experience.

So, using the CBT tools available, including setting up virtual labs using VM Ware or Hyper-V is a good training tool for those kinds of exams.

But, in order to answer the essay and other kinds of exam questions, there is a proven method to get better and quicker results.

To underscore how best to approach these kinds of problems, let's do some math.

A Mathematic Word Problem Being Used as an Instructional Tool to Provide a Logical Strategy to Answer an Essay Question for a Certification Exam – or - Show Me the Money

Mathematics problems train us to look for the key elements of a problem, and then use our knowledge of arithmetic to follow a set of logical instructions to derive the answer.

Q: Solve for X

$$X = ((49*48) / .75))*2.99$$

You can perform the order of operations and do the math and get an answer that makes sense:

(49*48) = 2352

2352 divided by .75 = 3136

3136*2.99 = 9376.64

A: X =9376.64

So, we can all agree on this being a correct answer, because everyone who uses their pencil and paper, or a slide rule, or a calculator, or a spreadsheet ends up with the same answer.[28]

But putting the same information into a word problem will abstract this kind of calculation a bit:

> Q: How much would it cost to floor a rectangular warehouse manufacturing space whose dimensions are 48 feet wide, and 49 feet long, if the estimated cost for a ½" thick carbon-fiber / epoxy composite insulating tile that has an electrical resistance of 45,000 ohms / cm, measuring ¾ of a square foot in area is $2.99?[29]

This problem has the same information as the prior problem, but since it is obscured by the words, we now have to process just what exactly is the question being asked.

---

[28] Or they SHOULD...

[29] I can hear the screaming from here...

It is actually a problem in three parts – find out the area of a rectangle, find out how many smaller squares will fit into the area of that rectangle, and multiply the number of squares by a cost of 2.99.

We need to break the problem into these parts, in order to get the answer to the question –

How much does it cost for all that flooring?[30]

What are the steps we will now perform to understand and answer the question?

---

[30] *We are omitting the manufacturing, transportation, and installation costs for simplicity in this example, as well as the fluctuating price of a barrel of oil that is necessary to creating the cross-polymerization of the fibers that comprise the actual tile materials themselves. Also, we assume standard pressure and temperature conditions, to achieve a hypothetical ideal state.* Everything in *italics* in that prior sentence has absolutely NO bearing on the correct answer. Watch out for diversionary language!!! Identify the KEY CONCEPTS, and know exactly what is the real question being asked.

1) What is the area of a rectangular box that is 48 feet x 49 feet?

(48 * 49) = 2352 square feet

2) How many tiles would be needed to cover that area with a floor if each tile is .75 square feet?

2352 divided by .75 = 3136

3) How much would it cost to cover the floor of the rectangle if the tiles are $2.99 cents each?

3136*2.99 = 9376.64

A: $9376.64

The answers are the same, on the surface.

Many people have difficulty in isolating the key information in the second instance, and that is why the technique we just performed will give better results.

By isolating and breaking the problem into manageable parts, and solving each one in turn, the anxiety level can be vastly reduced.

This approach also provides an easy way to check your answers by performing the operations in reverse.

The final idea to grasp here is that a lot of the words in that question were irrelevant to actually FINDING an answer.

Yet, this is how information is presented in the certification exams, as well as many times in the working world. Too much information (data) can obfuscate the real problems needing solved, just as thoroughly as having too little information.

Knowing what is important to solving the problem and what is not is a key skill to develop.

And, it takes practice.

In the IT certification arena, one way to get that practice is CBT, and it is relatively inexpensive. [31]

---

[31] In an upcoming section, I will provide more detail regarding CBT.

You only need provide the time to learn the material, and then take the exam.

Using CBT trains you to identify which terms and definitions are meaningful, and the context in which they present themselves during an exam.

Most CBT simulation software does a remarkable job of looking and feeling like the actual test, and many incorporate the appearance and timers from the actual exam.

For example, Exam Cram™ and Prep-Logic™ prided themselves on having a large enough pool of test questions and also could track your progress as you repeated the simulation exams.

You can also download additional sample questions. You can tailor the exam to focus on only one area, selected areas, random questions or the entire pool of questions, depending on your preferences.

I used to take each section, and get to where I scored 100% on five repeated tries.

After that, I would test for the next section, until I again achieved a 100% score five times in a row.

I would then add in the prior section and take it until I got 100%.

Then I would move on to the remaining sections in turn, each time assuring a 100% score five times running, and then adding the earlier sections, until I could score 100% for the entire question pool. [32]

This meant that I could pick any section at random, or any question at random, and KNOW the answer, as given by that CBT test software.

Since I also would use a variety of software programs, I was presented with a total pool of questions that probably approximated between 75% - 100% of the actual body of questions that would actually present during an official examination, depending on which certification was being tested.

---

[32] If you are suspecting that this might have taken some amount of time, you are correct. As I mentioned in the beginning, I am not in the business of giving you the answers to the certification exams, this book is intended to give you proven methods to pass these exams. And this is a PROVEN method, although it takes effort. TANSTAAFL.

In some instances, an adaptive testing algorithm would stop the exam in as little as twenty out of a possible ninety questions.[33]

---

[33] Adaptive testing means that the exam will adjust quickly to your level of knowledge. It usually is about twenty five to thirty questions, but I have heard of as few as ten. Once you hit a passing score, the test is over, and you have passed - which is of course the desired outcome. I like it when the exam goes "Passing score achieved! Congratulations!" Especially when it is unexpected...

Methods to Prepare for the Certification Examination

My preferred method of study would depend on the complexity of the certification being sought.

The primary idea is to use a layered approach to studying the material.
You should explore what the certification domains actually test. You can do this by visiting the certification body website, and searching for criteria or other samples of test questions.

Once you have an idea of what is actually on the exam, you can then proceed to identify which areas you must study, the areas that are the ones one which you personally should focus, and those areas in which you are familiar.

Taking a preliminary test will help you to ascertain these accurately.

I like to gather the information, and then take one or two practice exams, just whipping through them as fast as possible.

I am not concerned with the score I get at this point. I am only familiarizing myself with the test domains, the phraseology and terminology, and what the exam may look like on test day.

The primary reason for this is to get over worrying about whether or not you know ALL of the information. You more than likely don't, irrespective of the amount of experience or 'book-learning' you may already have.

You are learning the topology of the particular test, not whether or not you are an 'expert' in this particular body of knowledge.

That comes much later.

Gathering of study material is a matter of budget, personal preference, access to resources such as an internet connection or computers, and time management.

You will need to prioritize which of these is most important in your study plan. For instance, you may have many manuals and texts available at your workplace, which can be loaned out to you.

If you have a corporate library, they may actually have CBT or other online portal access to facilitate your studies (on your own time, of course).

But make sure that you tailor your approach to your own particular circumstances, and create a study plan that makes sense for YOU.

In my particular case, I would identify a certification, and then take a personal inventory of what I did or did not know about the subject.

I could create a list of likely resources, and examine the criteria for the domains.

I would then map out my work experience to these domains, and decide where I needed to apply some extra effort.

So, if the exam was going to be on something in which I had substantial OJT or other experience, say for a programming language, then I might only buy a single text book or CBT software package.

In some cases, I would simply attend the training online, taking very good notes. Other times, I felt it was necessary to attend a boot camp to gain mastery in a short period of time.

Your particular situation will dictate what approach works best for you, but I recommend that you formalize this approach.

In other words, make notes about HOW you went about getting positioned to go after a particular certification.

Notice what skills you already have obtained in your career and map these to certifications where there is a higher probability of success.

One of the important things about IT is that more knowledge is almost always better.

The more situations to which you have exposed yourself, the more it shows potential employers (and current ones) that you are able to be a flexible asset.

Certifications provide objective proof that you are able to learn and APPLY the knowledge within certain narrow parameters.

But, this is a very good additional piece of information for the hiring manager to have, when you are competing with hundreds of other potential employees.

Once I had decided to pursue IT certifications, I took note of my approach to successfully completing the goal of passing them.[34]

---

[34] It is imperative that you set some kind of deadline. Most people seem to perform better when they are under some kind of time constraint. The major problem here is that this may not be under your control. Your employment situation may dictate you get certified NOW, or within a very short period of time. You will need to schedule the test itself. Since you can only sit the test for certain certifications once or twice a year (ISACA CISM is one of these) then you need to plan accordingly, both with time and money. This is of special concern if your employer is giving you financial assistance. Be sure to discuss this with your management as a condition of obtaining required certification.

In all cases, my particular regimen would go something like this:

- Decide on the certification
- Plan a time when I would take the exam
- Procure texts or other resources
- Begin testing, using CBT
- Take notes about the areas uncovered during CBT in which I was not as strong as I needed to be
- Refer to and highlight relevant areas in texts
- Update notes
- Draw Memory Maps, where applicable
- Use Index Cards to record terminology
- Listen to Audio books or videos, in the background, while reading the material
- Organize the material around the major domains and key ideas
- Continue taking the CBT until I would attain 100% scores on a given domain
- Advance to the next domain and repeat the process
- Append that domain to the CBT exam, take exam until 100% scores attained
- Repeat for all domains
- Update notes one final time
- Schedule and sit the exam

If I were attending a boot camp, all of this would occur after sitting through the lectures and other prepared materials and simulated exams. [35]

I have found that a great method to facilitate this style of learning is to use yellow legal pads.

For instance, for the ten domains of the CISSP, I purchased ten legal pads. [36] I used one pad for each of the ten domains, transferring my notes from the class into the relevant section.

I supplemented that information with additional cross-references from the CISSP manual, Shon Harris book, and boot camp materials. [37]

---

[35] Boot camps are not for the faint of heart!

[36] Yours don't have to be yellow or even legal pads. You can use notebooks, or even a tabbed binder with loose leaf printer paper into which you have punched holes. Or separate binders. The idea is to have a physical location into which you store all the related information for that ONE section. If you look at the certification websites, or the printed material, it will identify these sections, (sometimes called DOMAINS.) Use one pad per domain.

By doing this, the information was centralized into a manageable set of sections, to which I could easily refer when doing my practice exams.

The other strategy that may not be evident here is HOW I approached the actual environment in which to study. Usually, I worked in quiet areas, without distraction.

Whether this was a kitchen table, or a library nook, the fact remained that for me, being able to work uninterrupted was a major item in maintaining the correct level of concentration.

I also try to not have Facebook, or a chat window, or Skype, or any other browser open UNLESS IT DIRECTLY APPLIES TO THE MATERIAL BEING STUDIED.

---

[37] Yes this is a LOT of effort, but recall that by doing all of this, I was able to pass on my first attempt. TANSTAAFL

PRO TIP:

Every time you are interrupted when working intensely, you will lose time regaining to the same point at which you were distracted.

You lose momentum, and your mind ends up having to pick up the thread of logic and information you were following in order to continue.

If this happens enough times, you will find you may end up starting over.

Therefore, it is imperative to inform people who may interrupt that you are working, and to leave you alone for some set period of time.

A good rule of thumb is to study intently for forty minutes, take a five minute break, resume studying for another thirty minutes, then break for ten minutes.

During the breaks, get up and stretch, refill your drink, and try to not be drawn into distracting discussions or situations.

Treat your study time seriously, and make sure that your roommate, spouse, etc. also realize you are serious by not being drawn away without VERY good reasons.

Pets, cell phones, texting and IM are all things that will try to get your attention by any means possible.

DON'T BE DISTRACTED!!

You may prefer a different environment, but the key idea to remember is that the closer your studying mimics the actual test environment, the less variables you need to worry about.

This is why loud music, (to which you will NOT be allowed to listen during the test) is not always a good thing to have when you are learning the test.

Now, you may study the materials quite handily with loud background music, but remember that the auditory cues you are subconsciously creating will be absent during the actual exam.

Another thing to watch out for is time getting away from you. Set an alarm clock to help you know when you need to take a scheduled break.

Tiring yourself when you study is a bad habit that leads to disinterest and boredom.

If you want to be successful in achieving this important goal, then you need to stay alert and concentrate on the material. If you become tired, be sure to take a rest.

Mark the point at which you are stopping, so that you can go immediately back to that place when you decide to continue.

Most of this seems very obvious, but there is a huge difference in knowing this in your mind, and actually setting out to do the research and preparation in a methodical way.

If you just sit down and begin studying bits of information at random, you may do well on test day.

However, I am pretty sure, based on my experience, that if you follow a logical, planned path of informational learning you will most assuredly pass.

Textbooks –

As an adjunct to self-paced training or boot camps, textbooks are one of those things to which you are going to want to pay some close attention.

The major issues with them are that specific information in PRINTED textbooks becomes dated with enough time. So, eventually, your then-new copy of Network Security Administrator's Guide for Solaris 2.6 will eventually be worth more as a paperweight.

Textbooks are expensive, even if you are shopping Barnes and Noble or Amazon.

Plus, there are usually shipping costs.

O'Reilly and Wrox offer e-book versions of their texts, and, since you are reading this e-book, you know that there is a lot of good information already out there in this format.

One advantage that paper still has over e-ink at this point is that the tactile learner can write in the margins of the book. [38]

Text books also used to occupy a place of honor on the shelves of the learned, as reference guides.[39]

Still, there are certain subjects that are more easily gleaned when using a text book.

So, choose wisely, and only pay what you need to pay. [40]

Textbooks tend to be very expensive, and can become outdated quickly, as has been noted.[41]

---

[38] I know, some people shudder at the thought of defacing a book, but this is because it was drilled into you as an impressionable child that you were NOT allowed to mark up the textbooks. The cheap administrators of your particular school system simply wanted to get as much use out of the texts as they possibly could. Don't worry. It's YOUR money and YOUR book now. You can set it on fire if you want. Please wait until after you pass, though.

[39] Today, with Google™ and the Internet, not so much.

[40] I don't think that second-hand or used books should be avoided, but examine them carefully. You don't want to buy a book that has notes that some other visual learner has scribbled all over, since they may not emphasize the same items as you.

Computer Based Training –

There is a plethora[42]of Computer Based Training software applications in the world for you to use as you pursue your path towards certification.

Some of the better known publishers are the Transcender™ series, Prep-Logic™ (now Learnsmart™), and Exam Cram™. These publishers offer DVDs and also online training options.

The typical package includes access to a pre-defined set of questions that are 'similar' to the actual exams.

Now, in the case of the CISSP and other essay-type exams, like ISO 27001, there is not a true direct correlation between the exam style and the actual exams.

---

[41] In my opinion, if you are seeking the CISSP, then purchasing Shon Harris' book is probably your single best bet. Buy it about six months before you sit the exam. Then READ it.

[42] Plethora is a fancy, two-dollar word that means "a LOT"

The CISSP is mainly a multiple choice or essay exam (although certain items may change as time goes one).

The ISO 27001 exam is completely an essay exam. The majority of other certifications for IT either are computer-based, offered through a testing center, or use simulators.

There had been some concern that the CBT modules replicated the exam experience TOO closely.

As a result of this concern, a lot of hiring managers were (rightfully) skeptical of candidates who had *certification disease*.

They reasoned that the certifications were essentially worthless, since anyone could spend a few weeks practicing to take the exam, sit it, and be reasonably sure of achieving a passing score.

So, anyone showing up with certs and little or no experience usually ended up wasting both their time and the manager's time.

Unfortunately, this tendency to not really understand exactly what the certification process was illuminating caused a lot of problems for qualified individuals as well.

Regarding my recent experiences speaking with hiring managers, there is still a tendency to look askance at certifications as not really having any true applicable value, or not map to real-world problems.[43]

In my opinion, the real value of certifications is three-fold:

- It shows commitment to the organization and a willingness to learn new methods
- It shows that the individual has a rudimentary grasp of terminology
- It shows that the individual values education

---

[43] A good way to educate an employer regarding the value of a given certification is to Google how well it is perceived across the industry. There are "Top Ten" lists published at various times by publications, and they indicate trends in acceptance of given certifications. I would present the opinion that if the US Government, Department of Defense, or other well-known organization accepts a cert, you can be fairly comfortable with its validity as an acceptable measure of competence.

So, the real problem comes down to this — is CBT a form of 'cheating'?

I personally do **not** find that the use of CBT is cheating.
The software I have used gave a good feel for the information, but it still was mainly a review of concepts I was already using in my day-to-day job.

The questions were not identical by any means.

Again, in my experience, the fact that one gets consistent 100% scores on a simulation exam does NOT guarantee that you will do the same under real-world testing conditions.

And, to be fair to the vendors of CBT, they are simply fulfilling a valid need — visual learners and tactile learners are well served by their wares.

A note about CBT — be sure to get authorized copies. There have been instances of malware versions being circulated for 'free'.

Online Learning –

Several times now I have participated in a remote learning experience, to attain a certification.

The key with this method is to take copious notes, and correspond with the instructor frequently.

While there are many technical challenges to overcome, (usually due to audio and video streaming limitations and bandwidth), the convenience of not having to travel is a very big factor for some.

My first experience with this method was in 2001, when I was getting a vendor specific certification, as well as an AIIM certification for Enterprise Content Management. My last AIIM certification was also an online experience, and the ECM Master class was a far cry from that first effort.

The first course was essentially a series of Powerpoint slides, with a quiz after each section (online) and a final exam.

The Master course required us to prepare a thesis from a Case Study. It was much more challenging and rigorous than pretty much anything I had done since Organic Chemistry. [44]

----

[44] I recently (August of 2012) participated in courses for ISO 27001, via the Internet. The course went well, and the material was presented professionally. I ended up with two large binders of printed material, anyway, since the exam was 'open-book'. The best part of this was that I did not have to drive anywhere when I was done for the day. The instructor kept things very lively, so that I did not feel like I was being ignored. This is an important consideration during boot camp type training of any stripe, incidentally.

Boot Camps

The best thing about boot camps is that they can be exciting, pressure filled challenging places to cram tons of material into your brain. You end up really feeling like you have run a marathon, and have accomplished something.

The worst thing about boot camps is, inevitably, the price associated with them, and the logistics of getting there and back.

Add to that the fact that they are typically 3 -14 days in length, and that you probably will have to use vacation time and your own money to go, plus the scheduling hassles, and it can be quite the experience.

I attended three boot camps, pretty much back-to-back, for my MCTS, CISSP, and CEH. I passed first time each time. I attribute that to both my excellent instructors, and my busting my ass for twelve hours a day, and sometimes more.

I came VERY prepared, I had years, and in some cases decades, of real-world experience and I brought audio books, CBT, and textbooks to them as well.

I had usually a good month of preparation using the material I already had BEFORE I even showed up to the boot camp.

And, yes, they are grueling.

You end up slogging through so much material that it almost doesn't even register.

When you have completed the exam, you usually have no idea how you did, unless it was a computer administered exam.[45]

My boot camp experiences have varied. I attended several in the late 1990's for SUN Solaris admin and network training.

---

[45] And then you may sit there wondering why you didn't pass. Your second thought is usually "get me the hell out of here!"

The facilities were in Orlando, Florida, and I stayed with relatives, so my living arrangements were comfortable. The classes were a mix of lecture and hands-on.

They were pretty damned hard, as well.

I remember that the company I was working for paid for all of them, but not all at once. I attended the first one, then several months later the second, then about a year later, the third. The facilities were well-appointed, and the labs were modern enough.

The second boot camp I attended was in Tallahassee, Florida. It was not on the same level as the first.

We attended the training in State buildings that were not really designed for comfort of learning.

The equipment had some technical problems. The instructor was not feeling all that well.

I passed that one as well.

But, it provides some contrast with the first experience, in that I was working for a different organization at that point.

Also, there was a tremendous amount of wrangling that needed to be done for me to actually attend.

I did not get a definitive answer as to whether I could actually attend until the deadline for registration had almost passed.

The thing to watch out for here is that your organization may have budgetary constraints or other factors such as vacation (or if you are even allowed to go because of seniority issues).

This makes boot camps an iffy thing sometimes.

If you are attending on your own dime, and find, as I do, that they are the best way for you to learn and pass certification exams, then try to schedule them in areas or at times of the year with moderate weather.[46]

I enjoyed the boot camps, because you basically have access to all the learning facilities 24 hours a day, for the entire time you attend.

---

[46] Personally, I LOVE the snow. I drove a four-wheel drive truck through snow storms in the Poconos in December and had a blast! And, I passed the exam!

They provided snacks and drinks, and tea, coffee or soda, as well as healthy foods such as fruit, yogurt, and even Hot Pockets in some cases!

Yes, you are paying for all of these conveniences, but the major advantage is you do not really have to do anything OTHER than prepare for the exam.[47]

Even at the boot camps, once the formal study periods and lectures had ended, I would sequester myself in my villa, and break out the study materials on the dining room table.

I always had an audio book playing in the background, and would take a break to listen every so often.

This total immersion in the source material ends up paying huge dividends when it comes time to sit the exam.

---

[47] One other item to note – you may be able to take some deductions on your taxes, for educational purposes. Consult your accountant. Ask them about unreimbursed employee expenses, or education deductions if you work for someone else.

I recommend boot camps for anyone that wants to achieve certification NOW.

If you follow the tips and tricks listed later, you should do well.

Be sure to ask around, incidentally, as not all boot camps are created equal.[48]

---

[48] I prefer the Training Camp™. Their facilities in the Poconos are a fantastic place to learn and take exams. I say this having attended three separate camps there, and passing each certification the first time.

Audio Books –

Auditory learners can benefit greatly from the audio book versions of popular titles regarding IT certifications.

Prep Logic™ had a very good quality series that I found immensely useful for the CISSP.

It covered the ten domains in fairly comprehensive detail.

I would not say it was THE definitive item that allowed me to pass the first time I wrote the exam, but I did find it allowed me to 'study' in some unusual places[49], and while driving to the Poconos on the way up to the boot camp.

---

[49] It's nice to listen to something while soaking in a warm tub, while snow falls outside your villa window, and not feel guilty you are not 'studying'. I also used audio books for CEH.

One of the funnier elements of the audio book route is the mispronunciation of certain terminology, and sometimes this can be quite amusing.

You may hear familiar terms that are said in a manner that it is obvious that the person reading the questions has no idea what the terms mean. [50]

---

[50] One glaring example for me was the term "Gram – Leech – Bee – Lilly" for the Gramm Leach Bliley act.

Braindumps –

People tend to have a low opinion of Braindumps, as the information is spotty. Plus, you don't always get correct information.

With that in mind, there is something to be said about Google™. You can pretty much hunt up a huge amount of related information using Google™, and don't forget you can also use Google™ Books!

I admit to not spending a lot of time with these.

I did use a braindump for Security +, but ended up not sitting for the exam.

Since I had decided by then to go for the CISSP instead, the information from the dump contrasted too much with the **Shon Harris** material for that particular domain, I ended up not even using it.

Your mileage may vary with this one, so be sure to check the dump against other sources.

Since you aren't likely to take the notes with you to the exam anyway, you would probably spend your time more wisely in doing CBT or listening to audio books.

Or just Google™ stuff...but keep good notes!

Memory Maps -

A memory map is a method to use visual cues to reinforce and memorize complex information.[51]

To use it you create a set diagram and link various types of information to each other.[52]

- The key concept is in the middle of the map.
- As you think of related ideas, create branches off the main idea.
- Use only the words that are key in conveying the idea.
- Use symbols to which you can easily relate the ideas.
- Group and organize similar concepts.
- Use arrows or colors to show relationships.

---

[51] This technique first came to my attention from Tim Ferris book "The Four Hour Workweek".

[52] An excellent use of memory maps to understand PGP encryption can be found at the "How PGP Works" website.

Mnemonic Training –

There are a couple of ways to remember lists of items.

One way is to simply write the list enough times to memorize it.

This is of course very time consuming, and if you have a ton of information to process, may not be the most effective means of doing this.

It DOES work.[53]

But, it is a clunky way to approach the idea of learning content.

Sometimes there are concepts for which this just is the only way for the information to finally sink into your brain.

---

[53] Please refer to my story regarding my GED student.

For example, a friend of mine worked on the Apollo 11 Moon Landing, for NASA. [54] He told me that he had to take a course in electrical engineering that required that he be able to write a schematic of some piece of equipment.

As part of being able to continue to work on these types of instruments, he had to pass a test regarding the particulars of this one kind of device.

The diagram that he had to draw, in one pass, included all of the resistance, voltage, and current information for each piece of that equipment.

The schematic contained maybe two hundred parts, and he had to know EVERYTHING about each component - where it fit on the breadboard, what was its power requirements - all manner of minutia were to be represented on his finished drawing.

---

[54] I may be an old fart to you young whipper-snappers, but this guy was older than me! He introduced me to personal computers, programming, and integrated circuits. He bought a Radio Shack TRS-80 that used tape cassettes! He even had an AMIGA! He's gone now, but I really learned a lot from him. Thanks, Ernie!

His approach was simple: to break the diagram into logical components.

He separated the wire paths into one drawing. He drew that one drawing until he could draw it with no mistakes, continuously.

Then, he drew all of the resistors on another drawing, noting the amount of Ohms for which each one was rated.

He superimposed THAT drawing on the one of the wire paths.

Then he did all of the capacitors. He combined this drawing with the ones of the resistors and wire paths.

Then the diodes. Then the transistors.

He continued doing this for the potentiometers, switches, lamps, and every other electronic piece that went into creating this particular instrument.

Finally, he made a series of mnemonic codes that helped him keep the information straight in his mind.

He imagined that he was walking along the wire path, holding a bucket of electronic parts, so that when he arrived at a particular point on the walk, he could place the corresponding part in the proper location.

So, he drew the path, then the parts, and added the specifications for each part, and then imagined he was taking a walk through the device.

He could SEE the diagram on the paper, and if he got there in his imagination, he knew what he should 'see' in his mind. If the two were not congruent, he added the part or checked his diagram for accuracy.

On the day of the test, he signed in, sat down and started his diagram.

He spent four hours on that drawing, and it was 100% correct.

Now, the point here is that the amount of effort expended produced the desired outcome.

He needed to be able to understand a very complicated piece of electronic equipment to prove he had the skills to work on something that ended up being one of the greatest accomplishments in human history.

And, since he really wanted to be a part of that moment, he pushed himself to the limits of his capabilities. He rose to the occasion and succeeded.

The idea of walking a path, or building a memory palace, is also known as the **Method of Loci.**

The idea is to create a memorable experience whereby you can remember certain items with any degree of detail you choose.[55]

While this takes some practice, it is a fairly easy concept to grasp and use.

---

[55] The memory palace figures quite prominently in the Hannibal Lector novels of Thomas Harris.

Now, the limitations here really get down to time and whether you have a detail-oriented memory to begin with, but almost anyone can train themselves to this method.

The real trick is knowing when to use this as your best method of practice for an exam.

In the information security realm, one of the more difficult concepts to understand is the idea of key exchange. I am not going to go into detail here, but the idea is that a user of a cryptographic system has a public key and a private key that are used to encrypt sensitive information.

The information can also be digitally signed to provide evidence for non-repudiation.

The entire process is somewhat complicated by the use of validating entities known as certificate authorities.[56]

---

[56] This is how your credit card information is protected when you engage in online commerce.

Diagramming the intricacies of PKI encryption provides a good case for using the memory palace method of memorizing detailed information.

Another application I found for memory palace was in the identification of the various types of block cyphers.

Finally, everyone has differing methods for what items resonate for them, and are easy to remember.

For some people it may be animals, for another person, colors. Use what works for you.

◄ ❃ ►

Peg method

The Peg Method was championed by noted author Harry Lorayne[57] as a quick way to memorize lists of items.

In essence, you assign a number or letter relationship to a series of mental 'pegs' on which you hang ideas or concepts.

Most peg methods use the numbers 1-26 or the letters of the alphabet as their pegs.

The idea is to provide a mental storage space for items in the list.

---

[57] Harry Lorayne's book "The Memory Book" contains much more detail regarding specific memory techniques. Since I am providing an overview here, it would benefit the industrious student, or merely interested individual, to give it some attention.

And, peg systems can be used with the memory palace to significantly expand the amount of information you are able to recall - you could combine the Alphabet Peg system with the Loci system to accurately memorize up to 260 items of information (by attaching a 10-sequence memory link to the key image of each letter of the alphabet).

The idea to understand here is not that it is easy to do these memory exercises, or that you even need to do them, but that they are ways that you may be able to reduce the amount of recall anxiety you may experience during a test.

The trick to passing a test is to either know the information so completely that you have no problem answering each question, or to know enough about the material to make logical deductions and arrive at the correct answer.

In the first case, you can use these methods to cram your brain full of information, but with the difference that you will be developing a strong system for recalling vast amounts of information at will.

The second case allows you the latitude of being able to think through a problem, and use the information to which you have been exposed to arrive at a logical conclusion.

Both of these skills are important, and neither should be dismissed out of hand.

Depending on the certification being sought, one or the other may be adequate, but being able to move freely through both processes will give you added confidence on test day.

How to Take Notes Well –

Note taking can be a huge drag, and a time sink for most people.

After all, the information is already right there in front of you, so all you have to do is read it again, right?

Unfortunately, that will not necessarily help you in retaining the information. (There may be a small number of people who CAN read something once and retain it forever, but the majority of us do not have photographic memories.)

So, a method that I have found works for me is to take notes three times.

First, you read the material before a lecture or training class (such as in a boot camp). Skim the material, paying attention to items that are bold or italicized, or seem to warrant special attention in the text book or other printed materials. Highlight or underline items that seem unclear to you.[58]

Next, if you will be attending a lecture or video presentation, take notes by creating a heading that states the main idea being presented. Ask questions about those highlighted items, and don't be satisfied until you really understand the answer. [59]

For instance, if the subject matter is firewall configuration, then the main idea is firewalls. As the lecture proceeds, make note of the different concepts being discussed, and write them as sub-headers.

------

[58] I know, most people either highlight EVERYTHING, or they underline the key words, right? Why should you underline the things you **already** know? Use the highlighter to remind yourself of the questions you are going to ask to the instructor, so that you can understand the content better.

[59] Don't be shy...you are paying good money for this information, and it is the instructors' job to assure you get the concept clearly.

For our firewall example, this might fall into firewall rules, or firewall types, or the different ways firewalls examine data (packet inspection, etc.)

Write a few lines that encompass the ideas being presented:
ie -

> *"Firewalls are devices that provide a separation of various segments of a network. They can be used to isolate network traffic to in order to prevent infiltration of unauthorized programs, or to prevent access to unauthorized users. Firewalls can be used to inspect data for indication of software programs that may cause harm to a system."*

And so on...

Do this in a fairly easy way, paying attention to the lecture or presentation.

LISTEN to what is being said, and then try to rephrase it in your own words in your notes.

If tape recording is allowed, then do so, or if there is a video available after class that can be reviewed, be sure to use that resource as well.[60]

The idea here is to cement the information into your long term memory.

You do this by hearing and participating in the learning exercises, and by reforming the ideas into concepts that you understand.

Your putting notes to paper will give you a tactile reinforcement of the concepts, and your understanding will increase by virtue of your having to redefine the information and write it down.

Finally, after you have written down the preliminary version of your notes, you will take a clean notebook and rewrite the information one more time.

---

[60] Use of online resources is of course recommended. But, don't get carried away, and stick to the matter at hand, so stay off of your social network while studying. Or, schedule a break, and indulge in a bit of socializing, but then get back to seriously concentrating on the information.

THREE Notebooks? -

You should have three copies of the information at this point:

1) The original material
2) Your preliminary notes (the working copy)
3) Your final copy of notes

I have found that I sometimes will go through an additional step of creating a third notebook, if I feel the information will be very useful in my work.

This should be a nicely organized book, and may even serve as a reference source later in your career.[61]

---

[61] The advent of tablets, smart phones, netbooks and other portable electronic devices to store information, as well as provide access to online information might seem to make this idea obsolete, until you are in disaster recovery mode, with no electricity, and no batteries for a few days. Hurricane, anyone?

The best thing about this note-taking business is that you can also use these notes in combination with the above mentioned memory improvement methods to create your memory maps and peg relationships more easily.

You can even diagram them in your notebook for a quick refresher.

⊰ ❋ ⊱

Test Day –

Staying healthy is of paramount importance.

As the day of the exam approaches, take note of your physical condition. If you are feeling ill, or down, then it might be a good idea to reschedule for a different day.

Try to eat a balanced diet. This is not to say go ON a diet, or radically change your eating habits. Just do what you normally do when you are feeling well, and continue this before exam day.

Stay hydrated during the test. If you are allowed to take a break for a snack or drink, then do so. If you can have a bottle of water at the workstation or desk where you are working the test, then by all means have one and drink from it.

Aside from slaking your thirst, it allows you a moment to contemplate the situation, and respond in a more relaxed manner.

Bathroom breaks should be taken if you need to go. [62]

If you find yourself in gastric distress, or have an upset stomach, then make this known to the examiner.

You want to take the exam in as much comfort as you can manage.

Everyone gets off kilter once in a while, so don't feel ashamed if you suddenly have a case of Montezuma's revenge.

---

[62] Hey, we are all human, and there is nothing to be ashamed of here, nor ridiculed. This isn't kindergarten. But, by all means follow the proctor's instructions if you need to excuse yourself, since you do not want to be disqualified because of a procedural issue.

Strategies for Taking Tests

IF YOU:

KNOW THE MATERIAL COLD –

When you are taking a written exam, be sure to use all of the space and other tools allotted to you to your best advantage. You can usually write in the test booklet margins, (or on the back of the pages, if they are one-side printed.)

Essay exams ask you to answer a question by writing a logical explanation that uses the information given in the question to reach a conclusion.

If you are in an essay exam:

1. Read the question carefully.
2. Underline the key ideas being presented.
3. Double underline the key elements in the actual question itself.
4. Think about what your answer should be, and write down your reasons in a clear and concise fashion.
5. Number your reasons, and show how each one can be applied to the particular section of the question it addresses as to being a correct deduction.
6. Review the answers to assure you feel they make sense.
7. Write simply and clearly.

Sometimes, you are not allowed to make a mark on the test booklet.

In this case, you may be allowed a scratch pad or some other medium on which to make notes.

USE THEM.

(Remember, you are only being graded on the accuracy of your answers, and not necessarily the neatness of your work.)

Of course, the final answers should be presented in a legible manner so that the meaning of your answer is evident.

If you are given a calculator, USE IT.

Make sure to double check your answers to assure you are answering the correct question. (Everyone can fat-finger a key, and that can have disastrous consequences if your first answer in a complicated set of calculations is off.)

Since the exam is timed, you should also follow this checklist:

1. Go through the exam booklet and skim to see if there are any questions that are problematic in their phrasing.
2. Mark these questions for later review.
3. Do the questions you know
4. Move smoothly through the exam, and if you encounter a question that seems difficult, mark it and move on to the next one.
5. Return to marked questions, and answer them to the best of your ability.
6. If a question seems to contradict a prior answer you have made, review both questions, and look for other clues or indications regarding the logical answer.
7. If you finish with time to spare, take a small break, then review the exam answers.
8. Resist the urge to change any answers unless you are absolutely able to defend the new answer, and it is truly the better answer to the question.
9. Be sure to take a drink of water or juice if you are allowed to have snacks in the exam room.
10. Be sure to take a bathroom break, at least once, just for the ability to clear your mind and relax. (Also carefully follow instructions regarding the breaks and snacks.)

IF YOU:

KNOW THE MATERIAL WELL ENOUGH

Remember the goal is to PASS the exam. You may feel confident enough to tackle a test, even though you may not know the material at the "A+" level of knowledge.

A lot of exams use 70% as a passing grade. This gives you a bit of leverage in how to approach the exam.

If you are up against the gun, with respect to absolutely having to get the certification, then don't worry if you are not getting 100% on all the practice exams.

Try for at least an 85% passing grade, at minimum, and study areas ONLY where you are having trouble if you are not getting 85%.

The reason for this is using statistics and test dynamics as a tool to pass the exam.

The very real likelihood exists that, by overcoming the psychological barriers you have regarding test anxiety by preparing as thoroughly as you are able, given the constraints, you will still pass.

Much of the ability to do well on tests comes from a sense of having been exposed to the information in a manner that allows you to recall it easily.

Another factor to consider is that you may remember or be able to use partial knowledge to make correct deductions or inferences about the test questions. [63]

---

[63] One place you CANNOT do this is if you are getting certified as a SCUBA diver, or for any safety related certifications that may come with SCADA, firefighting, flight training, firearms training or any other area where life may be at risk. 100% is required for all of these, and you need to have mastery or you can be injured or cause others to be injured. This is one area where the techniques can apply for the didactic portion of a test, and you will find that you will do very well. However, your instructors will test your actual performance in these scenarios, and that is outside the scope of this book.

◄ ✳ ►

IF YOU:

KNOW 'SOME' OF THE MATERIAL

The best outcome is to achieve a passing score on the first attempt, and of course, that is the point of this entire book.

Sometimes, circumstances arise that prevent you from actually finishing all of the studying, exercises, and CBT you have gathered.

If you find you are in the position where you are not familiar with much of the material, it may be best to postpone the exam, if at all possible.

Even if you are just getting ready to take the test, you may be able to delay or reschedule the exam, even just later that same day.

Test anxiety may be caused by not being ready, insufficient rest, illness, or even last minute emergencies or stress that occur as you are going to sit the exam.

You may find when you sit down that you are unable to concentrate on the material or questions.

Try to not get upset at yourself if you are in this situation, since it's not the absolute worst thing that can happen to you.[64]

---

[64] I can think of things far worse than not passing an exam. Getting eaten alive by velociraptors comes to mind. However, since we have not perfected cloning technology at the time of this writing, you should be safe.

◄ ✳ ►

IF YOU:

ARE NOT SURE

Some tips regarding tests in general:

- When in doubt, Charlie out -- if you absolutely are stumped, pick "C". Statistical probabilities bear out that "C" is a good choice on a multiple choice test. [65]

- Best guess -- You can use process of elimination to narrow down your choices to the most likely.

- Two ALMOST identical answers, one of them is the correct one -- If you are reading two questions that are almost the same, with one being a positive and the other a negative, one of them is the correct answer.

- Process of elimination -- If you have a group of similar answers, and one of these things doesn't belong, that is probably the correct answer.[66]

---

[65] Unless there are only two answers, but then it's 50/50, so flip that mental coin!

There are strategy differences in physical vs electronic interfaces, such as taking a test on a computer and using an answer book.

For computer-based testing, such as Prometric™ or Pearson VUE™, there is something called adaptive testing.

The format of the test may contain multiple choices, calculations, and complex answers that allow several options to be selected.

In a physical paper test, the format may allow you to winnow out an answer by the simple expedient of crossing it out with a pencil.
But, in the computer environment, the persistence of an incorrect answer provides a psychological distraction.

It may not seem like a big thing, but by performing the act of crossing through an answer, you are providing physical feedback that key off of the tactile learning we spoke of earlier.

---

[66] Think "Sesame Street".

It also provides a concrete reminder that you have discarded that particular answer and allows you to concentrate on the next one without any issues.

You can mark answers on the exam for review, but you can't really 'cross them out'.

A method you can use is to write the question number on your scratch pad and then the corresponding letters or numbers of each answer.

Then cross **THOSE** out.

It's not as tangible as striking out a questionable answer with a pencil, but it will allow you some confidence that you are progressing through the exam in a logical fashion.

Computer Simulations –

For certain certifications, such as CCNA, you may be required to perform functions in a simulations laboratory.

This means that you will need to go through a set of tasks that will be measured almost immediately. If you do not perform the task correctly, such as setting up a router, you won't be able to proceed, or will take a hit on your score.

The best advice here is to set up and use the virtual machines that are provided by the various vendors to practice the skills until you are proficient.

This is a case where practical experience is very important, and the more of it you can amass, the better your outcome.

Although you CAN do this in a boot-camp environment, I would submit that your experience of repeatedly performing iterative tasks over a week or two would not necessarily translate to someone being perceived as an expert, if that is the **only** measure of their proficiency.

Unfortunately, having a boot camp cert for something like this might not be indicative of anything other than that you can be trained to perform a task in a week or two.

Take heart, however, in that there are several college programs that are integrating the use of VM simulator software into their curriculum.

This acceptance of the training method and certification in institutes of higher learning indicate that they are considered as a viable means of measuring your abilities.

Since a simulation exercise is usually a controlled experience, you can do best on a simulation exam through ardent practice.

When you are doing the simulation, take notes regarding which problems or scenarios are proving the most difficult for you to finish correctly, and then ask questions.

You can use online fora or other resources available to you, such as Google™, other professionals, and instructors.

Anecdotes –

In the interest of full disclosure, and to provide you with that all-important sense of perspective, I would like to indulge in a bit more autobiographical exposition regarding my particular experiences in the pursuit of IT certifications.

A+

The day I took my A+ is forever etched into my mind. I had studied arduously, and felt very comfortable in my abilities, since I was constantly nailing all the prep questions on the simulated exams.

I could answer EVERY ONE of the three hundred questions, in any order, in any subset, and ALWAYS got 100%.

So, I felt more than ready.

The A+ consisted of two exams, and I had chosen to take them back-to-back.

I set off for the test facility, which was adjacent to a bank. The facility opened at 9:00 am sharp, so I left with plenty of time to leisurely get signed in, and acclimated.

In fact, since I was going directly to work after the test, I made the effort to get there even earlier than necessary.

I arrived about 45 minutes ahead of schedule. I took this opportunity to locate the exact door I would need to enter, directly across from the bank entrance.

I walked back to my car, and proceeded to study some last minute details I imagined might be important to know. It began to rain, so I decided I should go stand next to the offices, since it would probably open soon.

Now, since my exam was scheduled for 9 am sharp, I of course assumed that the facility would be open at maybe a bit earlier, since there would be checking in, and validation of my identity and all that.

I was standing outside the door, and noticed a lizard on the wall of the bank building. Being a kind-hearted soul, I decided to catch the lizard and deposit it on a bush that bordered the entrance to the entire office complex.

This entailed me spending some time to chase the lizard until I caught it, then releasing it into 'the wild'.

I felt that I had done my good deed for the day, and continued to wait outside the test facility door. Now, as it turned out, they were running a bit late that day. Almost forty minutes.

During that time, I walked back and forth to the bank entrance, and around the little courtyard outside the testing facility, peering into the door to see if anyone had arrived.

About 9:45, a friendly local sheriff pulled up alongside the bank, and got out of his vehicle. I noticed this, and did not give it much thought, as I was becoming more concerned with the time.

I had told my boss I would be in before noon, and the delay in the test facility not opening was going to alter my schedule. [67]

Imagine my great surprise, then, when the deputy shouted out "You! Stand against the wall, and don't make any sudden moves!"

---

[67] I did not yet have a cell phone.

I was wearing sun glasses, and looked around to see to whom he was speaking.

When it became evident that I was the only other person around, I pointed at myself and said "Who, me???"

He repeated his command, his hand on his holstered weapon. He was quite agitated that I had the audacity to question his authority, so to speak.

I removed my glasses, and he told me not to move at all. I stood there, now looking at a fairly serious man with a gun, and wondering just what the hell was happening.

For the next half hour I followed his instructions carefully, to be sure. I produced my wallet, and identification, VERY SLOWLY.

I stood with my hands against the wall while he frisked me.[68]

---

[68] This was before the TSA.

He asked me repeatedly why I was there, what my intentions were, and why I was not inside the testing facility (now open) if I was there to take a test.

Many of the bank and test customers walked by and gave me dirty looks.

I was beginning to become a bit stressed out myself.

NOW, in addition to probably missing the scheduled time to sit for the test, I was in danger of being arrested for loitering!

Luckily, we were able to resolve the situation when a nice young lady came out from the test facility and asked my name. She apologized for being late, and the nice deputy then gave me back my belongings.

I am pretty sure he told me that, while trying to be humane regarding the lizard, I looked like a damned fool that might have been casing the bank for surveillance weaknesses.

Apparently, unknown to me, the bank had been robbed several times in the preceding weeks.

After admonishing me about the dangers of acting 'weird' outside of a bank, he left, and I then went in to take the two exams for my A+.

Which I 'PASSED'...

I would like to inform you that you will most likely NOT think very clearly in those conditions, regardless of how well you may have prepared.

In the years since, my career has allowed me the opportunity to build, maintain and repair personal computers and enterprise level servers, so I can confidently say that I do indeed have the practical skillset to back up my A+ cert.

I always made sure to avoid testing facilities with banks after that, however.

Document Management Vendor Certification –

During one of my periods of being an 'employee', I had to attain a certification for a particular vendor, now long absorbed by larger companies.

This particular cert had me traveling in a company car to Tallahassee, Florida, during the fiasco that surrounded the 2000 Presidential election.

I ended up studying at the offices where all the excitement was proceeding regarding which candidate would win the election, with the Florida Supreme court challenges being made. It was somewhat of a distraction, and the facilities themselves were not ideal.

There were technical difficulties with the networked servers and computers, and the instructor, (who was a very nice woman) was undergoing chemotherapy, and was in between treatments.

She was cheerful and professional, but to say she was distracted would be a kind way to put it.

The class was composed of other professionals who had waited for this particular one week training camp to be made available.

It had already been cancelled once, and I had to wait almost a year to be able to get into it again.

This created a very difficult situation at my workplace, in that this certification was seen as integral to my advancement, (and subsequent justification for a raise), and also to assure the powers that be that a qualified individual was administering the system.

The training budget for this effort was also controlled by legislative mandate, and if the money was not used in a given fiscal year, it had to be petitioned and allocated via a complicated process for the next available budget period.

This meant that I had BETTER pass this certification test the FIRST time, or it was going to be cause for consternation in many areas.

Luckily, everything worked out in that the brouhaha in Tallahassee was settled, I passed the exam, and the country was able to be governed by President George W. Bush for the next eight years.

❖

Vendor Certification Story Two –

This story is included just to show you that certification does not always lead in the direction you may expect.

I was working as a consultant for a bank IT department[69] just before the huge economic spiral of the sub-prime melt-down.

We were processing a huge amount of paper documents into electronic versions for the bank underwriters to examine so that the loans could be made appropriately.

I was asked to obtain certification for a very specific technology, and this led to three certifications from the vendor in their products. [70]

---

[69] Ironic, isn't it?

[70] The bank was willing to pay all expenses related to this, incidentally. Talk about a sweet deal, right?

The training sessions were broken into a two week class, another two week class, and a one week class.

So, five weeks of training on someone else's dime has a bit of responsibility attached to it, as you might suspect.

When I returned from the first session, it was almost a year until the second one. The next two were separated by about a month, since the last certification was on a new product that had just been released.

This newest product was integral to our project, and offered a somewhat more flexible programming method to perform work functions using a custom scripting language that was proprietary.

I was part of the first group to even sit the exam, let alone experience the instructional material. So, pretty much, we were beta testing their training class as it was being given.

I particularly enjoyed that week. The instructor was very good, funny, interesting, and it was one of those rare classes where everyone was knowledgeable about the material, and we all had the approximate level of expertise and skill for the work involved.

The class time went quickly, we were able to catch up with the instructors from the earlier pre-requisite courses, and a fun time was had by all each evening after class.

The punch line is that, soon after I received these certs that particular activity of the bank was terminated and the process shut down.

So, I decided it was time to move on.

It was one of those 'writing on the wall' situations.

Almost all of the key personnel were being transferred, or were moving onto other engagements.

Since I was a consultant at this point, it was not really any skin off of my nose to make a transition to another gig.

I had already fulfilled my part of the bargain by applying my knowledge from the first two certification trainings to their business problems.

They did not ask me to refund their money for the third certification since they were the ones who made the ultimate decision to regroup and end the process.

About two years later, those particular certifications were integral in me winning a contract for another large customer.

The main reason I won the contract was because I was one of the few people certified in that particular product that had real-world experience behind me.

So, I feel I can therefore present you with hard evidence that certifications are used in some engagements to gauge expertise.

For me, these certs were very valuable, and ended up assisting me in winning contracts for several years after I had obtained them.

CISSP -

I have three tales regarding pursuit of my CISSP.

Orlando Security Conference –

In the late 1990's, the company I worked for invited me and several of my co-workers to a conference regarding Information and Operational security for businesses involved with the US Government.

While the details of this conference were confidential, I would like to relate a personal observation as to just how much authority the CISSP commanded, even then.

One attendee was a well-known auditor, who had just then passed and received CISSP certification. This one fact consumed a lot of discussion in our group.

It became the centerpiece of ALL of this person's conversations, and the funny part, to me at least, was that everyone listened to the auditor solely on the strength of that cert!

From the first slide the auditor presented, the fact that they had attained their CISSP was made very clear.

Here was a person to be reckoned with!

It just seemed a bit incongruous to me:

> "Well, I did this and that, and I think you might do blah blah blah. I think that, since getting my CISSP, I now realize the importance of ….etc."

Mind you, this person was very knowledgeable BEFORE they got the CISSP.

It just was interesting how those letters after a name could convey authority.

SFISSA Study Group –

I have been a member of the Information System Security Association for a very long time.[71]

About nine years ago, we decided that it might behoove our members to set up a study group for the purpose of attaining CISSP certification.

We met informally, and used the rudimentary study materials that were then available.

---

[71] In fact, I am now a Fellow, and sat on the Board of Directors for the South Florida Chapter as the President in 2014.

Several things became evident after we had been meeting for a time:

- There was not really any ONE expert in the entire ten domains of the CISSP present.
- Many of our real-world experiences did not mirror the concepts being espoused in the materials we were using.
- CISSPs were forbidden to discuss specifics of the exam.[72]

We were mostly on our own.

We decided to give it our best shot, and after eight or nine weeks, a couple of our members sat the exam when it was scheduled late in the year.

Two passed, and one did not, if I recall correctly.

---

[72] You may notice that we still are.

The odd thing to me was the then-president of the chapter did not have a CISSP, nor any other IT cert. They had attended many SANS training courses, but had not sat the test.[73]

I ran across this phenomenon of taking training classes and not sitting for the actual exams many more times over the years.

There seems to be a tendency in some people to skate right up to the edge, but not actually follow through or actually finish the process.
I firmly believe that this is an issue of self-confidence.

It underscores that perception of certifications as being worthless, in some aspects.

I feel my pursuing and attaining certs has better prepared me for the challenges I encountered during my career.

---

[73] And I certainly do not want to infer that this person was stupid or incapable of being president! We put on several security conferences under their direction, that were well-received by the community at that time. In my humble opinion, this person could have easily passed the CISSP. They apparently did not feel it was necessary.

I suppose that some people fear any objective criticism of their abilities, and maybe by not actually sitting the test, they can avoid facing an uncomfortable interpretation of themselves.

◄ ✱ ►

Bushkill Training Camp –

Disclosure: I would like to go on record that I have thoroughly enjoyed my experiences with The Training Camp™ in Bushkill, Pennsylvania.

This obviously biases my position on their particular boot camps, but I really want you, the reader, to understand just why this is.

In attempting three very different certifications, I have passed the first time EVERY time.[74]

The instructors were all well-known in their respective fields, the accommodations were very comfortable, the learning labs were impeccable, and the entire operation was run professionally from registration to certification.

---

[74] ASP.NET MCTS, CISSP, CEH

The Training Camp™ provided a complete experience. You had to do nothing but study. There was a lunch every day. Snacks, tea, soda, coffee, and fruit juices and fruit, pastries, and even Hot Pockets and yogurt were available 24/7 for the entire stay.

Class sizes were well managed, the instructors stayed on task, presenting a huge amount of structured information in a very short time.

There was a genuine camaraderie amongst the students, and each course offered its unique challenges. (I took my first class in December, and ended up dealing with snow!)

The CISSP course I took was in June, and the exam was at the end of a grueling seven day class.

This was one of the hardest exams I had ever experienced, and I went into it as prepared as anyone could possibly be, save having the actual answers printed out for them to copy.[75]

---

[75] THAT is what I would consider cheating, for your edification.

After I was done, I had this profound sense of relief that the whole ordeal was over. Coupled with that feeling was the thought that, if I did not pass, I would probably never take it again.

The combination of mental and physical exhaustion I experienced for the next week was unlike anything I had ever felt before. I kept wondering if I had answered everything in the correct manner, and would remember some obscure bit of trivia that convinced me I had definitely screwed the pooch.

When the email came saying I had passed, it was anticlimactic. I had climbed the mountain, seen the elephant, ate the mushroom, and knew that the actual score, whether I had passed or not, was somewhat irrelevant.

It was the act of being there, and actually steeling myself for something of that magnitude that made the biggest impression of my own view of my actual capabilities.

I did not need a piece of paper to tell me what I already knew anymore.

But, in retrospect, it sure was nice to know I had passed the **first** time!

Correlation to Real Problems

A very good question is how certification relates to real-world experience and problem solving.

In other words, is it just a piece of paper?

Or, put another way, do you really understand the subject well enough to be considered an 'expert' in whatever?

As I mentioned above, many times I was required to obtain certifications to provide a piece of paper stating what I already knew.

This was just a bureaucratic requirement for me to be able to 'prove' this knowledge. If I had to pay for the certification, it was one thing, but if the organization footed the bill, why not take advantage of the opportunity?

I feel that the certifications I have achieved during my career, taken as a whole, have only reflected my abilities I already knew I possessed.

They provided prospective clients or employers with evidence of my sincerity about staying abreast of technology.

Some may argue that you can buy or even print fake certificates, so that certs are suspect and worthless.

I personally don't see it that way.

I have been able to command very good rates, well above the average, when it was evident that these certs were not paper tigers.

I would caution anyone that achieving a certification does not mean you can slack off.[76]

But, you need to be able to sit back and count your victories, once in a while.

_____

[76] Quite the opposite, as I hope is evident by the necessity of continuing education.

Having amassed a stack of certifications, recognized around the world in the professional circles you inhabit, is a pretty cool thing to have accomplished.

The Certification Game

Certifications are used as filtering mechanisms by the Human Resources departments of most companies.

In most job descriptions, they typically are listed as the **minimum** criteria by hiring managers for potential hires to have.

A very real problem regarding certification paths is how current the information provided and tested really is.

For instance, the A+ certification came out at a time when the configuration and construction of personal computers mean understanding arcane things such as interrupts, DIP switches, and IRQ settings. Even though these are still concepts that are important, the typical technician today uses pre-defined tools that will configure the PC automatically.

Another situation is the rise of smart cell phones and other information devices such as the IPad.

These devices did not exist at the time the original A+ certification was implemented.

The relevance of the information being tested is one of the factors that make **staying** certified an expensive game.

As companies produce more complicated and sophisticated products, certifications for the legacy versions of these products become naturally outdated.

However, someone who has invested tens of thousands of dollars into a given certification that finds it is no longer relevant may become reluctant to invest even more money into a current cert.

Microsoft™ has a tendency to move fairly rapidly with its products, for instance.
And an MCSE in NT 4.0 or Windows 2000 is not going to favorably compare to the current flavor of MCITP.

Additionally, companies that offer training to maintain your skills rarely will pay for you to take certification classes.

They may provide for a stipend, or time off to take the test, or even have a method to reimburse you for the cost of the **test**, but will not usually spring for a boot camp.[77]

This cycle of creating a new product, and then a new certification for that product, can become infuriating, if you cannot manage to complete one cert before the next one is introduced.

For instance, Microsoft™ again had certifications to become an MCSE in Windows NT 4, 2000 Server, 2003 Server, and 2008 Server over a period of roughly twelve years (1996 through 2008).

This breaks down into four potential MCSE certifications in twelve years, or approximately having to recertify every three years.

---

[77] If you are fortunate enough to be in a situation where your company does offer some kind of educational reimbursement, it is definitely in your best interest to take as much training as they will allow. Aside from the obvious benefit of becoming certified, it shows you have initiative. Be careful to discuss your career path with your employer, so you do not become over-qualified, however.

The CISSP has a mandated refresh of every three years, unless a very large amount of continuing education credits can be obtained during that time period.

Plan accordingly.

If you are managing several certifications at once, try to space them out so you won't get slammed, either financially or as regards your time.

Continuing Education

Many certifications have an expiration date.

To maintain your standing in the community, you must prove your continued interest and expertise by either re-certifying (ie take the exam again) or by submitting Continuous Education credits.

These are called by other names as well, but essentially boil down to having taken the time to stay informed of the latest trends or items of interest in the field.

Some ways to obtain CE credits are:

- Read an article in a professional journal and pass a short quiz on the material. (This may be submitted via snail mail)
- Take an online quiz as offered by the professional journal

- Attend a seminar about the particular information technology
- Write articles or books and publish them in a recognized professional journal
- Teach or train others in a formal setting
- Give a presentation about the information during a professional organization meeting

While the number of CE's required to stay current varies, most certification bodies indicate that this requirement is pretty much the best way to maintain the relevance of your certification.

You may have to only enter the amount and date of a given CE to the professional organization via a website portal, but the organization usually reserves the right to audit you for evidence of you having completed these.

Therefore, it is best to keep some manner of permanent record to support your additional training.

Passing and Failing

Some people who take certifications exams pride themselves on having achieved 100% scores.

To be fair, this is indeed an indication of perseverance and dedication. It also might mean they were just lucky that particular day.

Having said that, the goal of any test is to give a measure of what you do know regarding the particular material being tested.

There are some certifications that will NOT tell you a score.

In fact, you will never get a score from them, nor will anyone else.

They follow a structured approach that allows for a PASS or FAIL outcome.

This also can be frustrating if, when you do not pass, you are not really sure WHY.

You may believe that you were pretty close to passing, when in actuality you were not.

Regardless, the real goal here is to PASS the exam.

If you are in a competitive work group, the scores of each person being known may lead to undue tensions, or favoritism.[78]

The use of CBT can assist in determining the areas of study where you need more work, but they are not able to properly simulate all of the conditions on a given test day.[79]

----

[78] It may also be the case that a particular individual is a natural test-taker, and still not really be able to perform in an exemplary fashion on a given job. But that is beyond the scope of this discussion.

[79] Refer to the Anecdote section for some examples of factors that may affect you when you are taking a test.

In my own experience, boot camps are the closest to giving a sense of the stress or pressures that may be expected when sitting an exam.

A good instructor assures that the time spent in the camp is maintained at a decent pace, and usually takes different learning styles into account. That being said, they are also on a schedule, which adds the sense of urgency some require.

Self-paced study will give a good idea of your readiness to approach the exam if you are very honest about your own abilities. This is not always an easy thing to achieve.

Many people over-estimate their readiness, not realizing that a 90 minute proctored test in front of a computer, with or without notes, does not approximate the environment of their office or home study area.

The Goal Is To *Pass*

Remember – passing the test is really the only goal, and ultimately the one that counts.

◄ ❈ ►

BUT -

If you do not pass, this is not a reflection on you as a person.

It only measures your capability to pass that particular set of questions on that particular day.

You may have had extenuating circumstances that led to you not performing as well as you might have.

Don't beat yourself up.

Learning is a process.

The purpose of you picking up this book and reading it is not to get you to become certified without any work on your part, it is to teach you ways to **learn** more readily, and how to apply that information during an exam.

Learning material well enough to become expert at it takes **TIME**.

Apply the techniques you have learned here to identify the factors that may had led to your making mistakes, then go try again.

You are not stupid, a moron, or a loser because you failed one test. (Or even if you fail a lot of them.)

There is no reason to expect that you are perfect, and won't make mistakes.

Regardless of what you think others perception of you is as a result of this one exam, you are still someone who tried to do something that almost anyone would find difficult.

This is not the same as the rote memorization of grade school, it is testing your ability to perform and think in a specific set of circumstances.

And, you have learned a lot about yourself in the process.

You now know what you must study and on which areas to focus more effort so that you will be successful the next time.

If you look at it objectively, there are almost 7 billion people on Earth.

There have probably been closer to one hundred billion alive during your life time.[80]

Statistically, if one MILLION people have sat for that particular exam (and that is pretty unlikely) you are one of the 0.0001% who even had the opportunity to sit for the test!

And, you WILL eventually pass it if you are persistent and motivated.[81]

---

[80] http://what-if.xkcd.com/9/

[81] Personal admission – I had to take Calculus 2 four times before I actually passed the course with a "C+". I dropped out twice, audited it once, and then buckled down and passed it because I finally was motivated properly. I had to pay for all four tries, and only was reimbursed for the last attempt. I then went on to take Calc 3, Differential Equations and Statistics at the Bachelor's level, and then Linear Algebra, Discrete Math, and Logical Structures at Master's level, and passed first try on each. This is not because I am a math genius. It is because I learned how to study math to be able to understand the concepts and apply them to these subjects.

I Passed, Now What?

So, now that you have passed...

CONGRATULATIONS!

Now what?

Well, if you needed this to meet some requirement of your current job, then you now have the certification and evidence that your employer was wanting you to get.

If you are taking the exam for personal satisfaction or to enrich your knowledge, you now have evidence that you have been able to understand and apply the information in a particular set of circumstances.

If you are seeking employment, you may now honestly include the certification in your resume.
You can also include logos on your marketing material, (but more about that in a minute).

You are now part of the 'elite', people who have taken that god-forsaken test, and passed!

You should feel a measure of pride that you have completed this next step in your career.

However –

- Don't expect a sudden raise.
- Don't think this might have made you a whole lot smarter than you were.
- Don't use your knew found super-certification powers as a bludgeon around the office.
- People may not appreciate your ability.
- Or, they may sarcastically refer to your being "some expert" derisively if you make a mistake.

Unfortunately, there are still office politics, favoritism, jealousy and the whole range of human emotions with which to deal.

Don't sweat the small stuff.[82]

---

[82] There are certain things in life which you cannot control, and prime among them is other's feelings for you. You have only one life to lead, so you should do things that make YOU happy. **This is probably the most important lesson you will get from this book.** Having a piece of paper, or a gold star, or a gazillion dollars won't make you any happier after a point. Good relationships are far more important to prolonged happiness, in my opinion. If people are celebrating your victories with you, no matter how large or small, then you are achieving your main goal in life – to be happy and move down your own path. People who place obstacles in that path are not intent on doing you any favors. You owe them nothing. Not your deference, not your respect, and not even your pity. If they persist in being an obstacle to your happiness, you only really have one choice in this regard. Ignore them, their opinions, and their insistence on making you Unhappy, and move on.

Marketing Tips –

Be sure to prominently display your accomplishments on your business card and any other correspondence, such as email signatures or marketing brochures.

Always use officially sanctioned logos that are provided by the certification bodies, and adhere to their standards for properly displaying these logos.

These are certainly badges of honor.

You can also just insert the acronym for the certification after your name.

This can become a bit unwieldy after you have amassed five or six of these, so be sure to use good judgment in choosing just which certs will grace your business card.

My personal rule of thumb is to only use the logos of certs that have returned on your investment of time and money.

⋖ ✳ ⋗

Financial Aid Options

I would not recommend going into debt for ANY certification. (Nor any college degree, for that matter.)

While CBT, self-paced learning, and study groups won't pound your pocket book too much, boot camps are notorious for providing financial aid or financing that may be a bit of a stretch.

Don't assume that getting any certification is a 'golden ticket' to riches.

Having a certification doesn't guarantee anything.

If you ARE NOT employed:

Although there are usually financial aid options available, be VERY cautious about using them.

Understand the terms of repayment, the interest rate, and the true cost of the training.

You may be able to look around and find programs that will assist in your pursuit of getting certified, or strike a deal with a potential employer in exchange for certifications.

If you ARE employed:

If at all possible, get your employer to pay for the training.

You can phrase the argument regarding your obtaining a certification in many ways, but all they will want to know is what the Return On Investment for them is going to be.

Now, this is not a bad problem for you to have.

All the salary surveys, apocryphal tales, and other stories about how much money you are suddenly going to be making should be taken with a large grain of salt.

Having said that, knowing the value of a particular certification can be empowering if you find yourself in negotiating some perks, or a raise, and you happen to be the only person that actually has one.

Successful negotiation depends on a lot of things, such as the mood of your boss, the timing of the financial cycle, and whether your other work performance can supply evidence of an increase in your salary.

You will need to quantify the value added by your certification.

Perhaps they can now use your certification as support for some program or project that they have been pursuing, and your expertise in that area will assure success for them.

Perhaps you are willing to train other personnel or produce some kind of training documentation to assist the company in achieving its goals.

You are the best judge of how to identify opportunities where your skills can be best utilized, and how to sell their value to your employer.

A word to the wise – if your employer has paid for the certification, they probably won't see a need to increase your salary until you demonstrate that their 'investment' is paying big dividends over non-certified personnel.

You sometimes are better off to simply enjoy the sense of accomplishment and professional recognition you have achieved by getting your cert.

And, sometimes, it is just another check in the box that needed to be completed.

Take some comfort in reflecting on a job well done.

⊰ ✳ ⊱

Final Thoughts

You should now have a pretty fair idea of how to go about determining which certification path is good for you.

You have some new understanding of what it is all about.

You have some pretty powerful tools to use to make it happen.

I would love to hear from you if you have applied these tips and tricks and decided that they worked for you, or didn't.

Please contact me at the following email:

cellichw@ccsproductions.com

Good Luck on That Exam!

◄ ✳ ►

Resources

AIIM - Enterprise Content Management / ERM / BI

http://www.aiim.org/

Checkpoint - Firewall

https://www.checkpoint.com/services/education/certification/index.html

Cisco – CCNA / CCIE

http://www.cisco.com/web/learning/le3/le2/le0/le9/learning_certification_type_home.html

CompTIA – A+, Network +, Security +

http://certification.comptia.org/home.aspx

Certified Wireless Network Professional

http://www.cwnp.com/certifications/

EC-Council – CEH / LPT / CHFI

http://www.eccouncil.org/courses/certified_ethical_hacker.aspx

Resources (cont'd)

ISACA – CISA, CISM, CRISC

https://www.isaca.org/Pages/default.aspx

isc2 - CISSP

https://www.isc2.org/

Juniper

https://www.juniper.net/us/en/training/certification/

Linux Professional Institute

https://www.lpi.org/linux-certifications

Microsoft Certifications

https://www.microsoft.com/learning/en/us/certification/cert-default.aspx

ISO 27001

https://mycima.net/

SANS – GSEC / GIAC / GPEN

https://www.sans.org/

Index

Bibliography:
Works Cited

Visual XE "Visual" , *Auditory* XE "Auditory" , *and Kinesthetic*
XE "Kinesthetic" *Learning Styles (VAK)*. (2011, July
12). Retrieved August 29, 2012, from Visual, Auditory,
and Kinesthetic Learning Styles (VAK):
http://nwlink.com/~donclark/hrd/styles/vakt.html

Defense, Department of. (2012, January 24).
http://iase.disa.mil/eta/iawip/content_pages/iabaseli
ne.html. Retrieved September 02, 2012, from DISA:
http://iase.disa.mil/eta/iawip/content_pages/iabaseli
ne.html

About the Author –

William A. Cellich has had a varied and interesting career.
A man of many talents, he has been involved with technology, film and information technology since the early 1980's.

Having an inquisitive mind and a creative eye for detail, Mr. Cellich began creating animated films on Super 8mm film in the early 1970's.
He made his first animated film, "Space Wars", four years before George Lucas' "Star Wars" hit the big screen. It can be seen on YouTube here, along with other early efforts.

In 2008, he entered a film contest for "Chiller TV". Titled "Sunday Dinner", it portrays a creepy look at a bizarre situation. He wrote, directed, acted, did special FX, and scored this short video.

A recognized expert in information security, Mr. Cellich is a Fellow of the Information System Security Association, and is President of the South Florida chapter of ISSA.

He has written many articles on various subjects.

He worked on many advanced aerospace engines, including the ones for the F-14, F-15, F-16, the SR-71 Blackbird, the RL-10 rocket engine, the Space Shuttle SSME, the F-22 and F-35 military jet fighters, and other classified projects. His work led to patents for methods of cleaning F-100 engines.

He has five beautiful daughters, no pets, and loves riding motorcycles, target shooting, fishing, and other outdoors activities.

Mr. Cellich is available to speak on a variety of subjects.

E-Mail: cellichw@ccsproductions.com

www.ingramcontent.com/pod-product-compliance
Lightning Source LLC
Chambersburg PA
CBHW051238050326
40689CB00007B/969